THE LIFE OF LEWIS CARROLL

Lewis Carroll

THE LIFE OF LEWIS CARROLL

BY
LANGFORD REED

W. & G. FOYLE, LTD.
"AT THE SIGN OF THE TREFOILE"
LONDON

This, the First Edition
Published May, 1932

MADE AND PRINTED IN GREAT BRITAIN BY PURNELL AND SONS
PAULTON (SOMERSET) AND LONDON

THE CENTENARY OF LEWIS CARROLL

January 27th, 1932

I STOOD beside a humble tomb,
Set on a Surrey hill-side, where
The gorse was gay with golden bloom;
And heard a devotee declare:
"If Lewis Carroll *lived* to-day,
He'd be a hundred years, they say!"

And are his arts but mortal arts?
And can his knell be ever rung,
Who lives within ten million hearts,
And helps to keep them gay and young?
More mystical than mortal, he
Beholds his own Centenary.

For he, in that enchanted land
Ruled by Titania, best of queens,
Was born, and by her Royal command
Did visit these terrestrial scenes,
As her ambassador on earth,
To bring us fairy charm and mirth.

And thus, predestined to success,
He made the children's hearts respond,
And two great nations coalesce,
In one appreciative bond,
Which nought can cancel or confuse,
Made by the magic of his Muse.

His statue decks no city square,
With mediocrities in stone,
Whose pompous and pretentious air,
Evokes the contumelious groan;
The works he wrought shall represent
His meritorious monument.

If monument he needs, whose spell,
Our fancies to his fantasie
Shall everlastingly compel;
And so this thought occurs to me:
Beneath those white memorial stones—
Lie merely C. L. Dodgson's bones!

L.R.

FOREWORD

VERY few people, I imagine, would feel disposed to deny my contention that the personality of England's greatest and most popular humorist is probably less known than that of any famous literary Englishman since Shakespeare.

His characters have become national figures, and his phrases part of our every-day language, but the man, himself, is so unfamiliar that the average well-read Briton, who could tell you that the elder Dumas had negroid hair, and that Mark Twain smoked a corn-cob pipe, and give some account of their characteristics and appearance as well as of their writings, would be utterly at a loss on the subject of Lewis Carroll—after he had informed you that he had always understood that his real name was Dodgson—although familiar with "Alice in Wonderland" and its sequel from childhood.

It is largely due to Professor [1] Dodgson, no doubt, that we have hitherto, known so little of Mr. Carroll, and partly explains why a "Life and Letters of Lewis Carroll", written by a relative of the family some thirty years ago and now out of print, tells us very little about him, although I hasten to make acknowledgement in respect of valuable

[1] I am aware that he bore no official title of Professor, but as he was one, to all intents and purposes, I make no apology for so designating him.

9

information about ancestry I have been glad to use and with reference to extracts from two of its many interesting letters.

As explained to me by a close relative of Lewis Carroll, the singular reticence displayed in this work with regard to his personality may also be traced to the fact that, on account of his extraordinary solicitude for them, as well as for his literary gifts, his sisters regarded him with almost reverential affection, so that "it would have been impossible, while any of them lived, for any of the younger generation to even suggest that he *might* have had human failings."

I do not pretend that this present work is complete. It is, for example, little concerned with C. L. Dodgson—much as I envy his erudition and his mathematical talents—partly because I am not greatly interested in the subject and partly because it is one which could be better handled by a more "academic" pen than mine.

But I do venture to believe that I have rendered some service, both to the literary student and to the general reader, by revealing the personality, characteristics, sayings and doings of Lewis Carroll so intimately and comprehensively that he no longer be a stranger among his countrymen and among the countless admirers of his works in America. If, at the same time, I have contrived to be entertaining, I shall have achieved something accomplished by few biographers.

For the valuable co-operation which has been

given me in connection with the many unpublished letters I have been privileged to examine and quote, and in respect of "personal reminiscences and recollections" which have been offered me, I have to express my gratitude and thanks to Major C. H. W. Dodgson, Professor B. J. Collingwood (nephews of Lewis Carroll), Miss F. Menella Dodgson (niece), Miss Edith Craig, Mrs. Eden (formerly Miss Scott-Gatty), Miss Irene Vanbrugh, Mrs. Barclay (formerly Miss Isa Bowman), Mrs. Morton, Mrs. Spens, Miss Vera Beringer, Mrs. Alice Collet, Mrs. Nora Macfarlan, Miss Mary Brown, Mr. Falconer Madan, M.A. (former Bodley's Librarian at Oxford), Mr. J. W. Gordon, K.C., Mr. Bert Coote, the Rev. W. H. Draper, Mr. Alfred S. Harvey, and others acknowledged elsewhere in this biography, and I am also indebted to Messrs. Ernest Benn, Ltd., for permission to reproduce for publication the four photographs facing pages 25, 33, 36 and 55, respectively, and to Messrs. Macmillan for the same privilege in connection with Sir John Tenniel's sketches of the "Duchess" and "Humpty Dumpty," and one or two brief extracts from Lewis Carroll's writings.

I have also to express my regrets to other kind people whose letters I have been unable to use on account of their absence of specific details of incident or information.

If there be any other former friends of Lewis Carroll with appropriate, informative, and specific reminiscences of him, who feel they ought to have been represented in this work, I hope they will do me the favour of communicating with me in order that such omission may be rectified in any subsequent edition.

LANGFORD REED.

21, Christchurch Road,
    Hampstead Heath,
        London, N.W.3.

CONTENTS

CHAPTER I

PAGE

ANCESTRY AND EARLY CHILDHOOD 19

CHAPTER II

HIS FIRST STORY—"THE RECTORY UMBRELLA" AND ITS EDITOR
—AT RUGBY SCHOOL—A PROPHECY OF GREATNESS—THE
INFLUENCE OF DICKENS 27

CHAPTER III

STUDENT DAYS AT OXFORD—HIS TALENT FOR PHOTOGRAPHY—
SCHOLASTIC TRIUMPHS—THE BEGINNING OF "LEWIS CARROLL"
—FRIENDSHIPS WITH THE GREAT—TENNYSON'S NONSENSE VERSE 32

CHAPTER IV

THE LIDDELL FAMILY—THE BIRTH OF "ALICE IN WONDERLAND"—
ITS ASSOCIATION WITH LLANDUDNO—"THROUGH THE LOOKING
GLASS" 39

CHAPTER V

"THE HUNTING OF THE SNARK"—INVENTING CROSS-WORD PUZZLES
—THE "SYLVIE AND BRUNO" RHYMES—"FEEDING THE MIND" . 51

CHAPTER VI

PAGE

Lewis Carroll's Child Friends—A "Looking Glass" Letter—
Behind the Scenes 59

CHAPTER VII

The Reminiscences of Isa Bowman—Lewis Carroll's Foibles
and Fancies—Shocked by "Ta-ra-ra-boom de-ay"—His Love
for the Theatre 68

CHAPTER VIII

The Letters to Ellen Terry—A Scheme for Training Stage
Novitiates—"The Jabberwock" and the Tichborne Trial . 80

CHAPTER IX

Lewis Carroll and Love—His Dislike of Babies—His Jealousy—
Why He Never Married—His Talent as an Art and Dramatic
Critic—The Passing of Charles Lutwidge Dodgson . . 88

CHAPTER X

Lewis Carroll and his Religion—His Unorthodoxy—His
Views on Sacred Subjects in the Theatre, on Humour in the
Pulpit, Casuistry, Heaven, Hell and Total Abstinence . . 102

CHAPTER XI

Lewis Carroll's Place as the Founder of "Nonsense Literature" 111

CHAPTER XII

PAGE

"Nonsense Literature" Defined—Lewis Carroll's Technique
—His Designed Literary Humour and his Verbal Spontaneity 118

CHAPTER XIII

The Strange Case of Professor Dodgson and Mr. Carroll—
The Views of Tenniel and Furniss on Them—Complaining to
Carroll about Dodgson !—How the Former got his Ideas . 126

CHAPTER XIV

Lewis Carroll and America—The Record Sale of the "Alice"
Manuscript—"Alice" on the Cinema Screen—Epitaph . . 134

LIST OF ILLUSTRATIONS

FACING PAGE

LEWIS CARROLL . . . . *Frontispiece*

CROFT RECTORY 27

LEWIS CARROLL (aged 23) 32

THE ROSSETTI FAMILY (photographed by Lewis
Carroll) 36

ALICE LIDDELL (photographed by Lewis Carroll) . 39

METSY'S PORTRAIT OF "THE UGLY DUCHESS" . 45

LEWIS CARROLL'S STUDY 59

ISA BOWMAN 68

"GEORGIE" AND CARROLL DODGSON . . . 80

TENNIEL'S DRAWING OF THE DUCHESS . . . 88

TENNIEL'S DRAWING OF "HUMPTY DUMPTY" . . 118

THE FIRST TWO PAGES OF THE ORIGINAL "ALICE" MS. 134

THE LIFE OF LEWIS CARROLL

CHAPTER I

ANCESTRY AND EARLY CHILDHOOD

A STUDENT of heredity would find much food for reflection in the fact that for generations the heads of the Dodgson family have been literary parsons with a gift of whimsical humour. The great-great-grandfather of the subject of this biography held a Yorkshire vicarship in 1715, and his son, Charles, became Rector of Elsdon, Northumberland, in 1762.

Some idea of the latter's quaint and philosophic humour may be gathered from the following extract from a letter he wrote to his patron, the Duke of Northumberland, which also suggests that the life of a country clergyman in those days was very far from being one of comfort:

"Above the kitchen are two little beds joining to each other. The curate and his wife lay in one and the maid in the other. I lay in the parlour between two beds to keep me from being frozen to death, for, as we keep open house, the winds enter from every quarter and are apt to sweep into bed to me. If I were not assured by the best authority on earth that the world is to be destroyed by fire, I should conclude that the day of destruction is at hand, but brought on by means of an agent very different from that of heat. . . .

"I have lost the use of everything but my reason, though my head is entrenched in three night-caps and my throat, which is very bad, fortified by a pair of stockings twisted in the form of a cravat."

Later, the worthy parson became Bishop of Ossory and Ferns, in Ireland, and was afterwards translated to the See of Elphin. He was esteemed by George III for his learning and integrity. A number of his sermons were published in pamphlet form and are preserved in the British Museum. Anne, the eldest of his four children, married into the Lutwidge family, of Cumberland, and the only one of his three sons to live to manhood entered the Army and was assassinated during the Irish troubles of 1803. He left two sons, of whom the younger, Hassard, had a brilliant career at the Bar and became Master of the Court of Common Pleas. The elder son, Charles, who was born in Lanarkshire in 1800, restored the link between the family and the Church, and in many ways resembled his own distinguished son, now raised to the Immortals as Lewis Carroll.

Both were scholars of repute, who gained high mathematical and classical honours at Christ Church, Oxford, and were shy and reserved, and both possessed a strong vein of fanciful humour and a literary talent which found outlet in print.

In the case of the father, the whimsicality revealed itself mostly in conversation and anecdote, for apart from his translation of the writings of Tertulianus, the first of the Latin fathers, the dozen published treatises and pamphlets, of which he was the author, were all concerned with questions of theology or ethics.

As a result of two sermons on the subject of ritualism, which he preached in Ripon Cathedral after he had become an Archdeacon, on January 3rd, and January 17th, 1864, respectively, he had a bitter controversy with Dr. Goode, Dean of Ripon, who charged him before his Bishop with publicly preaching and teaching false doctrines. The Archdeacon's answer was to publish his sermons, and his defence of them, in a pamphlet which made a considerable sensation at the time.

In 1830 he married his first cousin, Frances Jane Lutwidge, the wedding being celebrated at Christ Church, Hull. Like her husband, she was descended from the Cumberland Lutwidges, concerning whose history very little information is available. The lady's father was Charles Lutwidge, who for forty years was Collector of Customs at Hull. He lived at No. 1, Charlotte Street, and it was from this house that Lewis Carroll's mother was married. Little is known about her, apart from the following description, placed upon record, many years later, by her distinguished son, who undoubtedly inherited from her his gentle and kindly disposition:

"She was one of the sweetest and gentlest women who ever lived, who to know was to love. The earnestness of her simple faith and love shone forth in all she did and said."

Although the Reverend Charles Dodgson was a rebel in respect of certain tenets of theology, he was a firm believer in practical obedience to Biblical injunction, at least so far as the New Testament was concerned, which he carried out so thoroughly with regard to the command, "Be fruitful and multiply" that his marriage was blessed with no fewer than eleven children, of whom Charles Lutwidge, the future Lewis Carroll, was the eldest.

The latter's introduction to the world occurred on January 27th, 1832, in the remote Cheshire village of Daresbury (seven miles from Warrington), of which parish the Reverend Mr. Dodgson had spiritual charge. In the Daresbury Registry of Baptisms, in the entry recording the christening of the infant, dated July 11th, 1832, the father is described as the Perpetual Curate of Newton Daresbury.

If there be anything in the suggestion of the gay and sprightly Beatrice in "Much Ado About Nothing," that terpsichorean liveliness on the part of the stars during a birth constitutes an augury that the new arrival on earth shall be blessed with a merry wit, there must have been a whole galaxy of dancing stars above the roof of Daresbury Parsonage on that night of January 27th. At least, it is wholly appropriate and pleasant to imagine so.

In those days the railway had hardly commenced to function, and much of the food and other necessities for the smaller provincial towns was conveyed by canal barges. On the canal which ran through one end of Daresbury village there was considerable traffic of this kind, and the good parson was so worried at the thought of the bargees and their families having no settled place of worship that he appealed to his wealthy neighbour, Sir Francis Egerton, for aid, with the result that one of the barges was transformed into a little church —the first of its kind I believe—and Mr. Dodgson used to preach there on Sunday evenings.

Daresbury was, and still is, one of the prettiest little villages in the north of England. Even to-day, according to the "A.B.C. Railway Guide," its population is barely one hundred. It stands on the main road to Chester, from the north, and the old-world peace which distinguished it a century ago has now, alas, been destroyed by the frequent honk of the motor-horn and the dust of continual traffic. The present church, which serves three other villages as well, only dates from 1851, but the fine old pulpit, in which Mr. Dodgson used to preach, is still preserved. Of the original parsonage only the gate posts remain.

In this secluded hamlet young Dodgson spent the first eleven years of his life, and in the delightful old English Garden of the parsonage made friends of caterpillars, snails and other queer creatures, and indulged his whimsical fancy by encouraging them to perform tricks, of a sort, and by giving them quaint personalities, prompted by their eccentric appearance. Years afterwards some of them lived again in the pages of "Alice," and have thus attained an immortality unequalled by no other denizens of the insect world, unless it be King Bruce's provokingly-patient spider.

The youngster also showed promise of the mathematical and mechanical talent which, though not pronounced enough to make the name of Charles Lutwidge Dodgson imperishable like that of Lewis Carroll, rendered it well known in his own generation, and proved that he was of those singular geniuses whom, in his own quaint phraseology, he would have described as a "portmanteau man"—that is to say, one man packed with two personalities.

An event which made a deep impression on his childish mind was a journey the family made to Beaumaris, where they had arranged to spend a much-needed holiday. The only means of transit was by stage coach, and the journey took three days, either way. It is to be hoped the parson and his little flock made this exhausting expedition in the summer, and that the summer was summer and not, as in these days, winter under another name!

Though Charles left Daresbury in his early boyhood, its charm and beauty made an indelible impression on him, as is proved by this description of it, in his poem, "Three Sunsets"[1]:

> I watch the drowsy night expire,
> And Fancy paints at my desire
> Her magic pictures in the fire.
> An island farm, 'midst seas of corn,
> Swayed by the wandering breath of morn,
> The happy spot where I was born.

[1] First published in "All the Year Round," in 1860.

Among the few visitors to the parsonage was the Reverend Mr. Bayne, headmaster of Warrington Grammar School, who occasionally took service for Mr. Dodgson. His son, Vere, and young Charles formed a friendship that became lifelong, and were afterwards fellow-students at Christ Church, Oxford.

In 1843, Mr. Dodgson became Rector of Croft, a village near Darlington, with a quaint old church which contained a Norman porch and an elaborate covered-in pew, which looked more like a four-post bedstead. [1]

The Rectory, a large brick house with red-tiled roof and tall chimneys, possessed a large and beautiful garden, and here young Dodgson dreamed and played and developed those two seemingly-opposite sides of his nature indicated by his talent for mathematics and his genius for nonsense, using the latter word not in its futile dictionary sense, but according to the more charming and popular significance which it has gained through the art of Lewis Carroll.

He invented ingenious and entertaining games, with rules which he elaborated with mathematical precision. One of these was a fascinating railway game for which he constructed a home-made train out of a wheel-barrow, a barrel and a small truck, which used to convey passengers from one station in the Rectory garden to another. At each station

---

[1] The ancient porch is still there and although most of the old pews have been replaced by modern ones, there remains one which answers to the above description. The Rectory is much the same, although the picturesque red tiles of its roof have been replaced by slates.

was a refreshment room and ticket office. As general manager of the line and its sole staff, Charles prepared the time-table and list of by-laws, collected the tickets and fulfilled a number of other offices.

His love for the drama, manifested throughout his life, was shown during these early years at Croft by the toy theatre and company of pasteboard puppets in colours, which he made with the assistance of the village carpenter. The figures were mounted on wood and controlled by wires, worked from above, and all the plays in which they stolidly appeared were written by young Dodgson. The original theatre is now in Mr. Creswell Brigham's Museum for Children at Darlington.

He was also a clever conjurer, and, arrayed in a dark wig and a white nightshirt, used to cause considerable surprise and delight on the occasion of parties at the Rectory, though his extreme shyness did not permit him to demonstrate his sleight of hand tricks outside its walls. It was at Croft, too, that he first displayed his very uncommon ability in the art of photography which, in after years, became one of the principal hobbies of this man of many talents.

CROFT RECTORY DURING LEWIS CARROLL'S BOYHOOD

CHAPTER II

ABOUT the year 1844, Mr. Dodgson was appointed examining chaplain to the Bishop of Ripon, and later became Archdeacon of Rich- mond (Yorkshire) and a Canon of Ripon Cathedral. In this year Charles, who had previously been educated at home, was sent to Richmond School. That he underwent the usual discomforts of the new boy is apparent in one of his letters to his parents, in which he said:

"The boys have played two tricks upon me. They first proposed to play at King of the Cobblers, and asked if I would be King, to which I agreed. Then they made me sit down, and sat on the ground in a circle near me and told me to say, 'Get to work,' which I did, and they immediately began kicking and knocking me on all sides. The next game was 'Peter the Red Lion,' for which they made a mark on a tombstone (we were playing in the churchyard) and one of the boys walked with his eyes shut, holding out his fingers, trying to touch the mark; then a little boy came forward to lead the rest and led a good many very near the mark; at last it was my turn; they told me to shut my eyes and the next moment I had my finger in the mouth of one of the boys."

It will be noticed that the partiality for paren-
thesis, which is so pronounced a characteristic of
all Lewis Carroll's writings, is here prominently
displayed.

It was at Richmond School, at the age of twelve,
that Charles wrote his first story, "The Unknown
One," which duly appeared in the school magazine.
The title suggests that, immature and confused
although its style must have been, the story had
something of the fantastic quality which distin-
guishes Lewis Carroll's adult writings, including
his letters. That his headmaster anticipated that
his young pupil might, one day, astonish the world
may be gathered from the following extract from
his first report upon him:

"I do not hesitate to express my opinion that he
possesses, along with other and natural endowments, a
very uncommon share of genius; he is capable of
acquirements and knowledge far beyond his years, while
his reason is so clear and so zealous of error, that he will
not rest satisfied without a most exact solution of whatever appears to him obscure. You may fairly anticipate
for him a bright career."

Before Charles left Richmond, he had commenced
the first of a series of amateur magazines, which he
edited during the holidays, for the diversion of the
inhabitants of Croft Rectory, including his eight
sisters. He wrote all the matter and drew all the
sketches for these hand-written journals, the most
ambitious of which he called "The Rectory
Umbrella."[1]

[1] The original magazine is now in the Harcourt Amory Collection of
Harvard College Library, U.S.A.

This ingenious journal appeared more or less regularly until 1853, and some of its literary matter was quite in the best Carrollian vein, particularly a skit on photography in which the young author prophesied that the photographer of the future would not only develop the exterior likenesses of his subject, but would be able to photograph their intellects as well, and to "develop" them from "negative" to "positive" mentalities.

At the age of fourteen, Charles was sent to Rugby School, becoming a pupil two years after the death of the great Doctor Arnold, immortalised in "Tom Brown's Schooldays."

At Rugby it would seem that the boy was not particularly happy, the fact that he had no liking for athletics and very little for the society of boys and, in respect of behaviour, was a model boy who worked hard and conscientiously and never ascended the winding staircase to the disciplinary chamber dreaded by so many of his schoolfellows, did not tend to make him generally popular. But though his natural shyness and gentleness of disposition, and the possession of so many sisters made him feel more at his ease in the company of girls, he was far from being a girlish boy, and on one occasion, at least, he engaged in fistic combat on behalf of a smaller boy who was being bullied.

In those days every new boy had to undergo the ordeal of mounting a table and singing a solo before his scoffing schoolfellows assembled for supper, under penalty of drinking a large mug of salt and water if he resisted or broke down.[1] How young Dodgson acquitted himself at this embarrassing ceremony has not been placed on record. But, looking back on the Rugby of his school days, many years later, he referred to the tyrannies practised on the smaller boys in the dormitories at night, and to the senseless custom among those in authority of imposing mechanical correction for minor breaches of discipline or behaviour, by compelling the delinquents to the unimproving transcription of hundreds of copies of some dull line from the classics which was supposed to contain a moral particularly applicable to the young.

The headmaster in those days was Dr. A. C. Tait, who afterwards became Archbishop of Canterbury. His opinion of his pupil's abilities was thus expressed in a letter to Archdeacon Dodgson:

"I must not allow your son to leave school without expressing to you the very high opinion I entertain of him. His mathematical knowledge is great for his age, and I doubt not he will do himself credit in classics; his examination for the Divinity Prize was one of the most creditable exhibitions I have ever seen."

While at Rugby, Charles read "David Copperfield," which was running as a serial in "The Penny Magazine." His opinion of it was thus expressed in a letter to his parents:

"I have read the first number of Dickens' new tale, 'Davy Copperfield.' It purports to be his life, and begins with his birth and childhood; it seems a poor

[1] See "Tom Brown's Schooldays."

plot, but some of the characters and scenes are good. One of the persons that amused me was a Mrs. Gummidge, a wretched, melancholy, person, who is always crying, happen what will, and whenever the fire smokes, or other trifling accident occurs, makes the remark with great bitterness and many tears, that she is a lone, lorn creature, and everything goes contrary with her."

Students of both Dickens and Carroll may trace a decided resemblance between Mrs. Gummidge and one of the tearful animals in "Alice in Wonderland."

Another of Dickens' books which interested young Dodgson was "Nicholas Nickleby," and during holiday-time he made a special coach trip, across forty miles of bleak and rugged moorland, to the village of Bowes, near Barnard Castle, to see the original of "Dotheboys Hall," a dismal, dilapidated building, tenanted by no living thing save rats and mice. The dreariness and ugliness of the village, in which the only person he seems to have encountered was a gaping idiot boy, so repelled him that he wrote in his diary: "Next to a prison or a lunatic asylum, preserve me from living at Bowes."

CHAPTER III

STUDENT DAYS AT OXFORD—HIS TALENT FOR
PHOTOGRAPHY—SCHOLASTIC   TRIUMPHS—THE
BEGINNING OF "LEWIS CARROLL"—FRIENDSHIPS
WITH THE GREAT—TENNYSON'S NONSENSE VERSE.

IN the spring of 1850 Charles matriculated, and
on January 24th, 1851, following in the footsteps of his father and great-grandfather, he became
an undergraduate at Christ Church College, Oxford,
and thus commenced a personal association with
it that lasted till his death, almost exactly forty-
seven years later. It is curious to observe how the
month of January seems to have been connected
with many of the most important events of his life.

His first year at Oxford was saddened by the
sudden death of his mother[1] and not even the
ardour with which he threw himself into his studies
could assuage his grief. In those days, Oxford undergraduates worked very much harder than they do
now. Charles rose at a quarter-past six and after
breakfast at seven and chapel at eight spent the
rest of the day in attending lectures and in
study, his particular subjects being Latin, Greek,

[1] Her letters, one or two of which I have been permitted to read, show
her to have been the most devoted of mothers who took the greatest pride
in the upbringing of her numerous children, and recorded the scholastic
achievements at Richmond and Rugby of her eldest, in a long list of his
many prizes, with explanatory details as to what they represented and
appeared to promise.

Lewis Carroll
(Aged about 23)

mathematics and divinity. Meals were served to the Christ Church men in Hall, a vast room contemporary with Cardinal Wolsey, the founder of the College, and containing his portrait and those of other historical celebrities. The food was served on pewter plates, and was of a kind no self-respecting undergraduate of to-day would tolerate, and the prices charged for it were outrageous. Soon after young Dodgson graduated, the Christ Church men put an end to this evil by taking control of the catering arrangements themselves, discharging the cook and butler and appointing a steward to supervise the service of those in the kitchen and check the various items of expenditure.

Charles' scholastic triumphs at Christ Church were many and rapid, and included the winning of the Boulter Scholarship, first-class honours in mathematics, second in classical moderations, and the degrees of Bachelor of Arts and Master of Arts in 1854 and 1856 respectively. He commenced his tutorial duties in October, 1855, and was soon given a regular appointment, as the following entry in his diary indicates:

"I am sitting alone in my bedroom this last night of the old year (1857) waiting for midnight. It has been the most eventful year of my life. I began it as a poor bachelor student, with no definite plans or expectations. I end it as a master and tutor in Christ Church, with an income of more than £300 a year, and the course of mathematical tuition marked out by God's providence for at least some years to come. Great mercies, great failings, time lost, talent misapplied —such has been my past year."

c

As a don, he worked even harder than he had done as an undergraduate, his normal working day being seldom less than eleven hours, of which seven were spent in lecturing and the rest in the necessary preparation for this and in teaching private pupils.

He first took up residence in Peckwater Quadrangle, but soon moved to the Great Quadrangle where most of the masters and the heads of the college lived with their families. His quarters were in that part of the Quadrangle known to every Christ Church man as "Tom Quad," and, at first, they were on the ground floor. But he soon transferred to the floor above, for it looked out upon the flat roof of the College, and it struck him that this was just the place on which to erect a studio for the practice of his great hobby photography. The necessary permission was soon granted and most of the leading lights of Oxford sat before his camera, as well as many of the distinguished visitors, during the next thirty years or so.

While still an undergraduate he had commenced his professional career as a literary humorist, during a vacation spent at Whitby, by writing a ballad and a short story which the present writer traced, not long ago, in old copies of "The Whitby Gazette" dated August 3rd, and September 7th, 1854, respectively. An extract from the latter appears elsewhere in this biography.

During a previous vacation spent at Ripon he met a remarkable woman who identified with prophetic accuracy the qualities and characteristics which were to make him famous. This was a Miss Anderson, a local clairvoyant, who claimed to be able to describe the character of any person, even if quite unknown to her, merely by holding a folded paper containing his or her handwriting. This was her delineation of the characteristics of the young student:

"Very clever head, a great deal of imitation; he would make a good actor, diffident, rather shy in general society; comes out in the home circle; rather obstinate, very clever; a great deal of concentration; very affectionate; a great deal of wit and humour; not much faculty for remembering events; fond of deep reading; imaginative; fond of reading poetry; may compose."

At Christmas, 1857, young Mr. Dodgson became editor of the University magazine, "College Rhymes" and later contributed several poems and articles to Edmund Yates' journals, "The Comic Times" and "The Train." It was now that he resolved to select a pen-name and after he had considered that of Dares, suggested by his birth-place, he took the advice of Yates and adopted the pseudonym of Lewis Carroll, which is based on variations of his real Christian names. Thus Lewis is developed from Ludovicus and Ludovicus from Lutwidge, while Carroll is merely an Anglicised form of Carolus, the Latin equivalent for Charles. His initial effort published under his now world-famous pseudonym was the long serious poem, "The Path of Roses," published in "The Train," in 1861.

That he was no great admirer of Yates' editorial
ability may be gathered from an extract in his
diary for August 13th, 1855, in which he refers
to the mediocrity of "The Comic Times" and
continues:

"I am not sure whether it would not be advisable to
raise its price to 2d. on the score of respectability or
lower it to a ½d. on the score of honesty."

Mr. Dodgson was ordained a clergyman on
December 22nd of this year by the Bishop of
Oxford, but the slight stammer[1] which marred his
diction, discouraged him from undertaking regular
clerical duties, though on the rare occasions when
he preached in the University Church his sermons
were models of lucidity and reason. There is an old
adage to the effect that misfortunes often prove
to be blessings in disguise, and it is highly probable
that had it not been for his stuttering tongue he
would have thrown himself so whole-heartedly into
regular clerical work that the "Alice" books would
never have been written.

His literary activities and personal charm gained
him the friendship of such distinguished people as
Tennyson, Ruskin, the Rossetti Family, Coventry
Patmore, Stuart Calverley, Millais, Holman Hunt,
Val Prinsep, Watts, Tom Taylor (author of "Still
Waters Run Deep" and other plays), the Terry
Family, Lord Salisbury, Professor Faraday, Mr.
Justice Denman and many others.

[1] A failing which affected every one of his brothers and sisters in some
degree and was, no doubt, a consequence of their parents' consanguineous
marriage.

MRS. ROSSETTI AND HER THREE CHILDREN, DANTE GABRIEL, CHRISTINA, AND WILLIAM

(Photographed by Lewis Carroll)

Many of these famous people were photographed by him, for this man of many parts had now developed such a talent for artistic photography that he could have made a good living as a professional photographer had he desired.

He first met Tennyson in 1856. A note in his diary records how the poet told him he had often dreamed long passages of poetry and believed them to be good at the time, though he could never remember them after waking, except four lines which he dreamed when six years old:

> May a cock sparrow
> Write to a barrow?
> I hope you'll excuse
> My infantile muse.

Another note in his diary, for May 9th, 1857, reads:

> "I breakfasted this morning with Fowler of Lincoln to meet Thackeray. I was most pleased with what I saw of him; his manner is simple and unaffected; he shows no anxiety to shine in conversation, though full of fun and anecdote when drawn out."

He first met Ruskin during the same year, and it was the latter who persuaded him to abandon his desire to develop his natural gift for drawing, by informing him that it was not pronounced enough for him to have any hope of becoming a successful artist.

All this time a curious and subtle change had been gradually taking place in his nature. The grave and studious boy, who had developed into a grave and studious young man, with no liking for any of the usual pleasures of youth, or for any form of physical exercise[1] save long solitary walks, began to exhibit a youthfulness of spirit which astonished and puzzled his relatives and adult friends. In truth, deep down in his heart, he was always half a child, but his childhood developed late, and it was not until he had reached manhood and had begun to encourage his other self—the mystical and fantastical Lewis Carroll half of his personality—that he commenced to enjoy his youth. And when the magic mood was upon him it was almost impossible for the prim and practical Mr. Dodgson to suppress it.

Fortunately for the world, Mr. Carroll's personality was stronger than the personality of Mr. Dodgson, so much so that, as I shall presently show, strangers who met him often recognised the former and ignored the latter.

[1] He used to relate that the only occasion on which he took part in a cricket match he was given a chance to bowl, but was taken off at the end of the over for inefficiency, the extent of which may be gathered from his statement that "I was informed that had my deliveries only gone far enough they would have been wides!"

ALICE LIDDELL

Photographed as a beggar girl by Lewis Carroll. Tennyson described this photograph as the most beautiful he had ever seen.

CHAPTER IV

THE LIDDELL FAMILY—THE BIRTH OF "ALICE IN WONDERLAND"—ITS ASSOCIATION WITH LLAN-DUDNO—"THROUGH THE LOOKING GLASS."

IT can hardly be doubted that a potential factor of the juvenescent transformation in the personality of Mr. Dodgson was his friendship with the three small daughters (and one of them in particular) of his friend and colleague Dr. Liddell, Dean of Christ Church,[1] who was a neighbour of his in the Great Quadrangle. There was something spiritual and elfin-like about the second child, Alice, which struck a gay and dulcet chord in the heart of the grave young don, the echo of which was destined to be heard by posterity long after the physical part of him was no more.

To amuse Alice and her sisters he wove the most wonderful fairy stories, full of the impossible happenings imaginative children love, and the eager appreciation and affection with which they repaid him inspired him, at length, to imperishable achievement.

It was on the morning of July 4th, 1862,[2] that there occurred that epochal expedition up the river

---

[1] Appointed 1855. He was co-perpetrator with Mr. R. Scott of that famous Greek-English lexicon which, since 1843, has been both a blessing and a bugbear to aspiring and perspiring students of the classics.

[2] As mentioned in his diary under that date.

to Godstow Bridge, with Lorina, Alice and Edith Liddell, when "Alice in Wonderland" first assumed story form. Alice Liddell was then about seven years old.

The first inception of the resultant masterpiece has been exquisitely described by its author in the verses which preface it. The final verse is surely proof enough that sweet Alice Liddell was Lewis Carroll's favourite of the three, and that for *her* he fashioned his immortal fantasy, although the beautiful poem which precedes the sequel to the story, "Through the Looking Glass," is addressed to the child reader:

> Child of the pure unclouded brow
>   And dreaming eyes of wonder!
> Though time be fleet, and I and thou
>   Are half a life asunder,
> Thy loving smile will surely hail
> The love gift of a fairy-tale.
>
> I have not seen thy sunny face,
>   Nor heard thy silver laughter;
> No thought of me shall find a place
>   In thy young life's hereafter—
> Enough that now thou wilt not fail
> To listen to my fairy-tale.
>
> A tale begun in other days,
>   When summer suns were glowing—
> A simple chime that served to time
>   The rhythm of our rowing—
> Whose echoes live in memory yet,
> Though envious years would say "forget."

It is pleasant to reflect that Lewis Carroll was wrong in his assumption that his little comrade would forget him. She remained his lifelong friend, and many years after the trip to Godstow, when she had become Mrs. Reginald Hargreaves, she wrote the following account of the scene:

"The beginning of 'Alice' was told me one summer afternoon when the sun was so hot that we landed in the meadows down the river, deserting the boat to take refuge in the only bit of shade to be found, which was under a newly-made hay-rick. Here from all three, came the old petition of 'Tell us a story,' and so began the ever-delightful tale. Sometimes to tease us—perhaps being really tired—Mr. Dodgson would stop suddenly and say, 'And that's all till next time.' 'Ah, but it is next time,' would be the exclamation from all three; and after some persuasion the story would start afresh. Another day, perhaps the story would begin in the boat, and Mr. Dodgson, in the middle of telling a thrilling adventure, would pretend to go fast asleep, to our great dismay. . . ."

In view of the very definite and authoritative data which exists as to the scene of "Alice's" first recital, it will surprise many people to know that there exists in Llandudno a fairly common belief that the story was written among the sand hills overlooking the Menai Straits, during visits made by the author to "Penmorfa," the holiday home of the Liddell Family, which was known locally as "Plas Dean," or The Dean's Palace, and is now an hotel.

In a courteous letter to the biographer, the Town Clerk of Llandudno says:

"I am inclined to think that Lewis Carroll spent more than one holiday in Llandudno. Several of the old inhabitants state that their parents had become acquainted with him during his stay with the Dean, and it is certain that time was prior to 1862."

I understand that Lewis Carroll's diaries contain only one reference about staying at "Penmorfa," but it is known that he paid several visits to Llandudno and loved to stroll and play with the children among the sand dunes on the west shore opposite the Straits. In those days they were much more extensive than they are to-day, and swarmed with rabbits. It is, therefore, highly probable that "the beginning of Alice" although first "told" at Godstow, on July 4th, 1862, was first imagined among the Llandudno sand hills, particularly when it is remembered that Alice's adventures commence with her invasion of the White Rabbit's burrow.

Lewis Carroll's association with Llandudno is commemorated by a street named after him, "Carroll Place," and by a font in the Church of Our Saviour, which stands in what used to be the centre of the dunes. According to the inscription on the tablet by the side of the memorial:—"The font in this church was the gift of children in memory of Lewis Carroll (C. L. Dodgson), author of 'Alice in Wonderland,' and a lover of Llandudno."

The original title of the story was "Alice's Adventures Underground," and before he had any thought of publication its author made a handwritten copy of it as a Christmas present for the living Alice. It was this small work of ninety-two pages which I saw sold at Sotheby's for the record sum of £15,400, as described in a later chapter.

It is not generally known that the story was first offered to the Oxford University Press and accepted. Two thousand copies were printed, but were withdrawn by the author, and sold in America, without any very definite reasons being given. He possessed so keenly the desire for beauty, which as Walter Pater says (in his essay on "Romanticism") "is a fixed element in every artistic organisation," that in later life he sacrificed a good deal of time and money to ensure that his books should be produced in a style which coincided with his aesthetic tastes. [1]

On the advice of his friend George Macdonald, the novelist and poet, author of that charming fantasy, "At the Back of the North Wind," the story was submitted to Messrs. Macmillan, who immediately appreciated its value and published it in 1865.

Few books have met with such unequivocal praise from the critics and such instantaneous favour from the public, and I feel sure that in any public enquiry into the popularity of children's books, either in Great Britain or America, "Alice in Wonderland" would come an easy first.

It has not only been translated into French, [2] German, Italian, Russian, Swedish, Spanish and

---

[1] See chapter XII.

[2] By Henri Bué, whose French-English "readers" and grammar were the best text-books of their kind in our fathers' young days, but who is possibly better remembered to-day for being the inventor of such instructive phrases, burlesqued by modern humorists, as "The pen of my aunt's gardener is larger than the pencil of the coachman's granddaughter."

Dutch—tasks which the peculiarly Anglo-Saxon nature of its appeal and humour must have rendered very difficult—but has received the distinction of official prohibition in China. This was in the Province of Hunan, whose Governor, General Ho Chien, in April, 1931, issued an edict prohibiting the use of the book among school-children on the grounds that to attribute the power of human language to beasts is an insult to the human race, and any children reading such books must inevitably regard animals and human beings on the same level, which would be disastrous!

Presumably the inhibition was to discourage translation, for I cannot discover any evidence of "Alice" having ever been printed in Chinese.

We must not blame his Celestial Excellency too severely. Even in comparatively enlightened England we have had a movement for expurgating fairy tales and nursery rhymes from the literature of the young, and replacing them with those appalling little "human" stories, infested with morals and precepts and totally devoid of humour, which are anathema to every healthy-minded child. The writers and exploiters of such drivel belong to that depressing school of practical pietists who would deny even the existence of humour in Heaven, despite the fact of the Creator having originated such jests upon earth as the chameleon, the earwig, the hippopotamus and the penguin![1]

---

[1] Which I suspect of having suggested to Mr. Charles Chaplin his world-famous walk.

METSY'S PORTRAIT OF THE "UGLY DUCHESS"

Sir John Tenniel's delightful drawings to "Alice in Wonderland" and its sequel have become nearly as well-known as the text, and are almost as imaginative. Not all of them are wholly original conceptions, however. For his studies of the Duchess he took as his model the famous portrait of the hideous Duchesss of Corinthia and Tyrol,[1] painted about the year 1520 by the Flemish artist, Quentin Metsys. The photograph of this, reproduced through the courtesy of Mr. Hugh Blaker, present owner of the painting, will show that Tenniel's adaptation was a pretty faithful one.

An account of a meeting with the author of "Alice in Wonderland" in Whitby, which was given in a letter written a year or two after the publication of the book, by a Mrs. Rennie, is worth quoting here, not only for the picture it presents of his thorough understanding of the childish heart and the reciprocity which always followed his friendly overtures to little children, but as showing how strangers could recognise the Carroll in him despite all the Dodgson denials.

At the hotel breakfast table, before her children and their nurse had made their appearance, Mrs. Rennie had encountered a distinguished-looking stranger, who had passed the usual compliments of the day with her and with other visitors but, otherwise, had seemed rather shy and reserved. After he had left the table the lady had remarked

[1] Born 1318, died 1369. Her tragic life-story has been told with great sympathy by Dr. Lion Feuchtwanger in his novel, "The Ugly Duchess."

to her sister that she felt sure the stranger must be someone of importance, and had been rallied on her imagination.

"Next morning (says her letter) nurse took our little twin daughters in front of the sea. I went out a short time afterwards and found them seated with my friend of the table, who was seated between them, with his knees covered with minute toys. They were listening to him open-mouthed and in the greatest state of enjoyment. Seeing their great delight, I motioned to him to go on and he did for some time. A most charming story he told them, about sea-urchins and ammonites. When it was over, I said, 'You must be the author of "Alice in Wonderland."' He laughed and said, 'My dear madam, my name is Dodgson and Alice's adventures was written by Lewis Carroll.' I replied, 'Then you must have borrowed the name, for only he could have told a story as you have just done.' After a little sparring, he admitted the fact."

Apart from the author of "Alice" himself, probably no one was more surprised at its success than Archdeacon Dodgson. The brilliant career he had hoped and planned for his talented son now threatened to be overshadowed by the genius of this hitherto unsuspected Mr. Carroll, and it is not too much to say that at the outset the good man was absolutely flabbergasted. But he was too broad-minded and too proud of his son's success to wish to handicap his literary efforts in any way and when he died, on June 21st, 1868,[1] it was with the knowledge that the name of Lewis Carroll would certainly be remembered by a grateful posterity.

[1] He was buried in Croft Churchyard in the same grave as his wife.

Soon after the publication of "Alice in Wonderland," its creator commenced work on "Sylvie and Bruno," which first took the form of a story entitled "Bruno's Revenge," which appeared in "Aunt Judy's Magazine," in 1867. The editor, Mrs. Gatty,[1] in accepting this, sent Mr. Carroll (as I now prefer to call him) the following letter:

"The story is delicious. It is beautiful and fantastic and child-like. Make it one of a series. You may have great mathematical ability but so have hundreds of others. This talent is peculiarly your own, and as an Englishman you are almost unique in possessing it. Some of the touches are so exquisite, one would have thought nothing short of intercourse with the fairies would have put them into your head."

Nevertheless, the story which eventually resulted gave him more trouble to write than anything he attempted, and was not finished until twenty years later.

In the autumn of the same year (1867) Lewis Carroll went on a Continental tour of some months duration with his Oxford friend, Canon Liddon.[2] His diary contains several amusing references to his experiences in Germany and Russia, of which the following are examples:

[1] Mrs. Alfred Gatty who (after her marriage to the Rev. Alfred Gatty, in 1839) wrote several books for children under her maiden name of Margaret Scott. She was the daughter of Nelson's friend and chaplain, the Rev. A. J. Scott, D.D. Her son, Alfred Scott-Gatty became Garter Principal King of Arms and was knighted, but is better remembered as the composer and writer of hundreds of songs and several plays for children. Her grandson, Alexander Scott-Gatty, is a well-known London actor.

[2] Henry Parry Liddon, 1829–1890. One of the ablest of the High Church party of his day, whose sermons at St. Paul's Cathedral, London (of which he was appointed Canon in 1870) attracted enormous interest.

July 23rd. (*Dantzig*): On our way to the station we came across the grandest instance of the "Majesty of Justice" that I have ever witnessed. A little boy was being taken to the magistrate, or to prison (probably for picking a pocket). The achievement of this feat had been entrusted to two soldiers in full uniform, who were solemnly marching, one in front of the poor little urchin and one behind, with bayonets fixed, of course, to be ready to charge in case he should attempt to escape.

August 6th. (*Nijni Novgorod*): We went to the Smernovaya (or some such name) Hotel, a truly villainous place, though, no doubt, the best in the town. The feeding was very good and everything else very bad. It was some consolation to find that as we sat at dinner we furnished a subject of the liveliest interest to six or seven waiters, all dressed in white tunics, belted at the waist, and white trousers, who ranged themselves in a row and gazed in a quite absorbed way at the collection of strange animals that were feeding before them. Now and then a twinge of conscience would seize them that they were, after all, not fulfilling the great object of life as waiters, and on these occasions they would all hurry to the end of the room, and refer to a great drawer which seemed to contain nothing but spoons and forks. When we asked for anything, they first looked at each other in an alarmed sort of way; then, when they had ascertained which understood the order best, they all followed his example, which was always to refer to the big drawer.

(*A few days later, at Kronstadt*) : Liddon had surrendered his overcoat early in the day, and we found it must be recovered from the waiting-maid, who talked only Russian, and as I had left the dictionary behind, and the little vocabulary did not contain *coat*, we were in some difficulty. Liddon began by exhibiting his coat, with much gesticulation, including the taking it half off. To our delight, she appeared to understand at once, left the room, and returned in a minute with—a large clothes brush. On this Liddon tried a further and more energetic demonstration; he took off his coat and laid it at her feet, pointed downwards (to intimate that in the lower regions was the object of his desire), smiled with an expression of the joy and gratitude with which he would receive it, and put the coat on again. Once more a gleam of intelligence lighted up the plain but expressive features of the young person; she was absent much longer this time, and when she returned, she brought, to our dismay, a large cushion and a pillow, and began to prepare the sofa for the nap that she now saw clearly was the thing the dumb gentleman wanted. A happy thought occurred to me, and I hastily drew a sketch representing Liddon, with one coat on, receiving a second and larger one from the hands of a benignant Russian peasant. The language of hieroglyphics succeeded where all other means had failed, and we returned to St. Petersburg with the humiliating knowledge that our standard of civilisation was now reduced to the level of ancient Nineveh.

In 1869, there appeared Lewis Carroll's collection of "Poems Grave and Gay," better known by its later title of "Phantasmagoria." By far the best thing in it was the very fantastic poem, in seven cantos, of 150 verses in all, in which a garrulous ghost recounts to a human being the habits, customs, woes and worries which specifically affect the various classes of beings in Ghostland, from the lordly spectres down to the homely phantoms. It is very ingenious nonsense, but above the heads of children, as the following verses, descriptive of the expense to which an ambitious ghost may be put, will show:

> For instance, take a Haunted Tower,
>   With skull, cross-bones, and sheet;
> Blue lights to burn (say) two an hour,
> Condensing lens of extra power,
>   And set of chains complete.

D

What with the things you have to hire—
  The fitting on the robe—
And testing all the coloured fire—
The outfit of itself would tire
  The patience of a Job!

Soon after the appearance of "Poems Grave and Gay," in response to the appeal of the Press and public, Lewis Carroll announced that he would write a sequel to "Alice in Wonderland." The publication of this was awaited in Great Britain and America with an eagerness and curiosity that was highly complimentary to its author, who after long and anxious toil to reach an assured but modest position as C. L. Dodgson, had achieved immediate fame as Lewis Carroll almost without an effort.

The new book, illustrated by Tenniel, appeared in 1871 and, for once, the expectations of the critics and the public were not disappointed. From the adult point of view, it is a better-written and more ingenious work than "Wonderland," particularly in respect of its parodies, and if for no other reason than its "Jabberwocky" ballad, than which nothing cleverer has been written in any language, deserves its immortality. Concerning this little masterpiece, its author has related that he composed it during an evening he spent with his cousins, the Misses Wilcox.

CHAPTER V

"THE HUNTING OF THE SNARK"—INVENTING CROSS-WORD PUZZLES—THE "SYLVIE AND BRUNO" RHYMES—"FEEDING THE MIND."

THE literary style of Lewis Carroll was now at its zenith, and for the next twenty-seven years his talented and prolific pen was constantly at work in the field of endeavour he had made peculiarly his own.

He devoted much time to developing "Sylvie and Bruno," and on the last night of 1872 related the fairy tale part of it to a number of children, including Princess Alice, who were members of a New Year's Eve party at Hatfield, where Mr. Carroll was the guest of Lord Salisbury.

During the next six or seven years, a number of small works from his pen were published, including his "Notes by an Oxford Chiel," which consisted of a series of whimsical essays which dealt with current Oxford controversies, and a long, serious article condemning vivisection, which appeared in the " Pall Mall Gazette."

And then in March, 1879, appeared his long nonsense ballad, "The Hunting of the Snark," which has enjoyed a sustained popularity only second to that of the "Alice" books. Many of his admirers

51

have contended that it is an allegory, but its creator always declared that it had no meaning at all, which, however, is very different from saying it has no point, for the meticulous skill with which each effect is achieved shows the master-hand throughout. The description, in half-a-dozen verses, of the characteristics of the "genuine warranted Snarks," is as delightfully nonsensical as "Jabberwocky" itself, as may be gathered by the following extract:

> Let us take them in order. The first is the taste,
>   Which is meagre and hollow, but crisp:
> Like a coat that is rather too tight in the waist;
>   With a flavour of "Will-of-the-Wisp".

Writing to Miss Mary Brown on the subject, on March 2nd, 1880, he said:

"I have a letter from you (received, I regret to say, August 27, '79) asking me 'Why don't you explain the Snark?' A question I ought to have answered long ago—let me, however, answer it now—'because I can't!' Are *you* able to explain things which you don't, yourself, understand?"

It is interesting to note that Henry Holiday, the brilliant artist who illustrated the book, made a drawing of the "Snark" which Lewis Carroll did not allow to appear. He explained that having made the creature "strictly unimaginable he desired him to remain so." The original drawing, I understand, is now in the possession of Messrs. Bumpus, the well-known Oxford Street booksellers.

Years after the book was published, in response for some rather more definite data as to the nature of the mysterious monster, than the ample but wholly incongruous description in the text, its author explained that the Snark was really a "portmanteau creature, partly a snake and partly a shark!"

In 1885 appeared "A Tangled Tale," in which Lewis Carroll combined mathematics and nonsense in a series of entertaining problems, and at the end of 1889, "Sylvie and Bruno," followed by its sequel, "Sylvie and Bruno Concluded," in 1893, and a year later by "Symbollic Logic," which the more mathematically-minded of Lewis Carroll's admirers possibly consider his best work.

In addition to his literary creations, the subject of this biography invented novel little puzzles and games, and an examination of some of the former suggests that he may have been the inventor of cross-word puzzles. Of the dozen or more books he wrote under his real name, several achieved considerable temporary success, particularly "Euclid and His Modern Rivals" (1882), which ran into eight editions.

It is not, however, with his famous works, or with the mathematical and much less-substantial triumphs of the more substantial Charles Lutwidge Dodgson that I now propose to deal. I prefer to introduce the reader to a new Lewis Carroll, or rather the old Lewis Carroll in new dress, in respect of extracts from letters and diaries and from lesser known works which are unfamiliar to the present generation.

Consider, for example, this entirely fanciful portrait from " College Rhymes " (1858):

MY FANCY

She has the bear's ethereal grace,
  The bland hyena's laugh,
The footsteps of the elephant,
  The neck of the giraffe;
I love her still, believe me,
  Though my heart its passion hides,
She's all my fancy painted her,
  But oh, *how much besides!*

Incidentally, this libellous lyric illustrates the lifelong and slightly-contemptuous attitude maintained by the confirmed bachelor who composed it towards the romantic affections. His first published tale (apart from the effort in his school magazine), "Wilhelm von Schmitz," which appeared in the " The Whitby Gazette," on September 7th, 1854, was entirely a lampoon on them. It contained several flashes of extravagant irony that gave promise of the rarer and kindlier humour which was destined to represent Lewis Carroll at his best. Its hero is thus described:

"He possessed a form which, once seen, could scarcely be forgotten. A slight tendency to obesity proved but a trifling drawback to the manly grace of his contour, and though the strict laws of beauty might, perhaps, have required a longer pair of legs to make up the proportion of his figure, and that his eyes should match

rather more exactly, yet to those critics who are un-
trammelled by any laws of taste—and there are many
such—to those who knew and esteemed his personal
character and believed that the power of his mind
transcended those of the age in which he lived—though
alas! none such as yet has appeared—to those he was
a very Apollo!"

But for the real gems among Lewis Carroll's
lesser-known works, one must examine those which
were published after he had come to his full powers
as a creator of reasoned nonsense with the "Alice"
books.

Who, to-day, reads "Sylvie and Bruno," and its
tiresome sequel? Even the generation in whose
age they were written grew weary of the task,
when it was discovered that something like three-
quarters of the four hundred pages comprising
each of these volumes consisted of a confused and
controversial sermon in the form of a novel which
was even more sentimental than the usual Victorian
romance. And the author never seems quite happy
in his portrayal of the character of Bruno, whom
he created as a concession to the popular appeal
that he should write a story round a boy. Bruno
is not like a boy—not even one from fairyland—
he is more like a roguish little girl pretending to
be a boy and speaking a language no boy would
speak, and at times, he becomes very irritating to
the reader.

Nevertheless, despite their many weaknesses, the
"Sylvie and Bruno" books contain two sets of
recurrent verses equal to anything in "Alice."

I refer to the Mad Gardener's rhymes and those describing the varied and bizarre accomplishments of "Little Birds." Here are two examples:

> He thought he saw a Banker's Clerk,
>   Descending from a bus;
> He looked again and found it was
>   A Hippopotamus:
> "If this should stay to dine," he said,
>   "There won't be much for us!"

> Little birds are writing
>   Interesting books,
>   To be read by cooks:
> Read, I say, not roasted—
> Letterpress, when toasted,
>   Loses its good looks.

The "Sylvie and Bruno" books also possess the distinction of claiming Carroll's most idealistic heroine, in the person of the half-fairy, half-mortal Sylvie, who is obviously intended to personify spiritual beauty, and is thus described in the final paragraph of "Sylvie and Bruno Concluded."

"Sylvie's sweet lips shaped themselves to reply, but her voice sounded faint and very far away. The vision was fast slipping from my eager gaze: but it seemed to me, in that last bewildering moment, that not Sylvie but an angel was looking out through those trustful brown eyes, and that not Sylvie's but an angel's voice was whispering: 'It is Love!'"

Undoubtedly a much more sentimental heroine than Alice!

There is excellent material to be found among

Lewis Carroll's scattered papers and the letters he loved to write to his child friends. Among the former is a rare work entitled, "Feeding the Mind," which was originally a lecture, given by him in October, 1884, in the parish hall of a Derbyshire vicarage, whose presiding parson was one of his greatest friends. Later, it was published in pamphlet form, but is so long out of print that I doubt whether I could have obtained a copy had not a gentleman in America, a stranger to me, who had been afforded some entertainment by one of my own nonsense books, paid me the graceful compliment of sending me a copy of the tiny volume in question. From it I extract the following:

It would fare but ill with many of us, if we were left to superintend our own digestion and circulation.

"Bless me!" one would say, "I forgot to wind up my heart this morning! To think that it has been standing still for the last three hours!"

"I can't walk with you this afternoon," a friend would say, "as I have no less than eleven dinners to digest. I had to let them stand over from last week, being so busy, and my doctor says he will not answer for the consequences if I wait any longer!"

Well it is, I say, for us that the consequences of neglecting the body can be clearly seen and felt; and it might be as well for some if the mind were equally visible and tangible—if we could take it to the doctor and hear its pulse beat.

"Why, what have you been doing with this mind, lately?" the doctor would say, "How have you fed it? It looks pale and the pulse is very slow."

"Well, doctor, it has not had much regular food, lately. I gave it a lot of sugar plums yesterday."

"Sugar plums! What kind?"

"Well, they were a parcel of conundrums, sir."

"Ah! I thought so. Now mind this: if you go on playing tricks like that, you'll spoil all its teeth and get laid up with mental indigestion. You must have nothing but the plainest reading for the next few days. No novels on any account."[1]

[1] For permission to make this extract I am indebted to the Rev. W. H. Draper the present holder of the copyright in "Feeding the Mind."

LEWIS CARROLL'S STUDY AT CHRIST CHURCH

CHAPTER VI

LEWIS CARROLL'S CHILD FRIENDS—A "LOOKING GLASS" LETTER—BEHIND THE SCENES.

SOME of the best nonsense by Lewis Carroll appeared in the amusing letters he sent to his child friends. Through one series, received by little Agnes and Amy Hughes, ran a fascinating fantasy about three thin cats, who slept between sheets of blotting paper, each with a pen-wiper as pillow, which is as original and entertaining as anything in "Alice"; but it is too long to reproduce here.

A letter received by Miss Jessie Sinclair, in 1876, comically details some of his preferences, thus:

"I like very much a little mustard with a bit of beef spread evenly under it; and I like brown sugar—only it should have some apple pudding mixed with it to keep it from being too sweet. I also like pins, only they should always have a cushion put round them to keep them warm. And I like two or three handfuls of hair, only they should always have a little girl's head beneath them to grow on, or else, whenever you open the door they get blown all over the room and then they get lost, you know."

Lewis Carroll, a life-long lover of the theatre, had many friends among London stage children who then, as now, were among the most fascinating and intelligent and best-mannered of youngsters. Occasionally he would invite parties of his small theatrical friends to visit him at Oxford, where he would entertain them delightfully, showing them the sights of the city, and describing these in a way that appealed to the childish heart, although it was more imaginative than veracious.

Sometimes he would concoct "looking-glass" letters, which could only be read by holding them up to the mirror, and in others he would begin at the bottom of the last page and write backwards, so that the only way to understand them was to read them in the same way. Here is an example, written to Miss Nellie Bowman, in 1891:

D. L. C.
    Uncle Loving Your,
.Instead grandson his to it give to had you that so, years 70 or 60 for it forgot you that was it pity a what and; him of fond so were you wonder don't I and, gentleman old nice very a was He .for it made you that *him* been have *must* it see you So .Grandfather my was, then *alive* was that 'Dodgson Uncle' only the, born was I before long was that see you then But .'Dodgson Uncle for pretty something make I'll now,' it began you when yourself to said you that, me telling her without, know I course of and; ago years many great a it made had you said She .me told Isa what from was It ?for meant was it who out made I how know you Do !Lasted has it well how and, Grandfather my for made had you antimicassar pretty that me give to you of nice so was it.
Nelle dear My,

Letters were not the only things upon which the fantastical humorist liked to experiment retrogressively. Several of his former child friends have told me of occasions on which he amused his small guests and himself by making some of his many musical boxes play backwards!

My friends Mrs. Barclay, Mrs. Spens and Mrs. Morton (formerly the three little Bowman sisters) and their youngest sister, Miss Empsie Bowman, were among the most intimate of these juvenile stage friends, and their regard for Lewis Carroll lasted till the day of his death. They received many characteristic letters from him. One of the most amusing, written to Miss Maggie Bowman, on September 17th, 1893, from 7, Lushington Road, Eastbourne, related a story about a basket containing 250 kittens and a sack stuffed with 500 pairs of gloves, which had been unexpectedly deposited (so the letter pretended) at the door of the Eastbourne house, and described how Mr. Carroll had carried the basket and the sack and their contents to the parish school, and presented them to the 250 little girl pupils:

"As soon as a kitten tried to scratch, it found all its paws popped into nice, soft, warm gloves! And then the kittens got quite nice-tempered and gentle and began purring again. And when any kitten wants to catch a mouse, it just takes off one of its gloves, and if it wants to catch two mice, it takes off two gloves: and if it wants to catch three mice, it takes off three gloves, and if it wants to catch four mice, it takes off all its gloves. But the moment they've caught the nice, they pop their gloves on again, because they know we can't love them without their gloves. For you see, 'gloves' have got 'love' inside them—there's none outside, you know."

Miss Bowman tells me a quaint story in connection with her visit to Oxford as the child actress playing the title role in the stage version of John Strange Winter's novel, "Bootles' Baby." It seems that one morning, when walking down the "High," accompanied by Lewis Carroll who had been showing her round some of the colleges, they met the Bishop of Oxford, who laughingly asked her what she thought of their famous city, and was much amused when, with true professional aplomb, the little actress replied: "I think it's the best place in the Provinces!"[1]

Mr. Bert Coote, the well-known London Actor, was another of Lewis Carroll's small thespian comrades. The acquaintance began in 1876, when Mr. Coote and his sister Carrie were members of the company of juvenile actors and actresses who for three years appeared in periodical seasons of pantomime matinées at the Adelphi Theatre, London. It was thus referred to in Mr. Dodgson's diary:

"Went up to town for the day and took E—— with me to the afternoon pantomime at the Adelphi, *Goody Two-Shoes*, acted entirely by children. It was a really charming performance. Little Bertie Coote, aged ten, was clown—a wonderfully clever little fellow— and Carrie Coote, aged about eight, was Columbine, a very pretty, graceful thing. In a few years time she will be just the child to act 'Alice,' if it is ever dramatised. The harlequin was a little girl named Gilchrist,[2] one

---

[1] Lewis Carroll mentions this incident in the ballad of twenty-seven verses, entitled "Maggie's Visit to Oxford," which he wrote to amuse his little friend, and which was afterwards published.

[2] Connie Gilchrist, afterwards the musical comedy star of the Gaiety Theatre, who, in 1892, married the Earl of Orkney.

of the most beautiful children in face and figure that I have ever seen. I must get an opportunity of photographing her. Little Bertie Coote, singing 'Hot Codlings,' was curiously like the pictures of Grimaldi."

"Mr. Dodgson often came behind the scenes," says Mr. Coote, "and all the children in the show adored him. I well remember my sisters, Carrie and Lizzie, and I spending a day with him at Oxford and being vastly entertained by his collection of elaborate mechanical toys. The autographed copies of his books and photographs which he gave me are among my most cherished possessions."

Another child comrade of Lewis Carroll was Miss Vera Beringer, with whose family he had become friendly after seeing the charming performance of the little girl, as she was then, in the title role of the stage version of "Little Lord Fauntleroy," in 1890. Here is a limerick he sent her, when she was spending a holiday in Manxland:

> There was a young lady of station,
> "I love man!" was her sole exclamation;
>   But when folks cried, "You flatter!"
>   She replied, "Oh, no matter,
> Isle of Man is the true explanation."

Miss Beringer tells me an amusing story which illustrates the slight absent-mindedness which was characteristic of Lewis Carroll. When he called one evening at her parents' house, where he had been invited to dinner, she heard a crash of metal in the hall a few moments after he had been admitted. Peering over the banisters to see what had happened,

Miss Beringer and her elder sister Esmé beheld the embarrassed visitor and the giggling servant-maid crawling about on their hands and knees, retrieving a pound's worth of silver and copper which Carroll had absent-mindedly accumulated in his breast pocket. On taking out his handkerchief to blow his nose, out had come most of the coins, which had rolled in every direction.

The absent-mindedness mentioned by Miss Beringer is further illustrated by the rather well-known story which relates how the subject of this biography once went to London to dine with a gentleman to whom he had only recently been introduced. Next morning he was stopped by this individual, while walking in the street. "I beg your pardon," said Lewis Carroll, "but you have the advantage of me. I do not remember ever having seen you before." "That is very strange," was the reply, "for I was your host last night!"

An amusing story which Major Dodgson tells me about his famous uncle's forgetfulness, and which he has always understood to be true, relates how Lewis Carroll went one afternoon to a house where he believed he had been invited to a children's party. He had no sooner been admitted than he dropped on his hands and knees and crawled into a room where a hubbub of voices suggested the party was in progress. Both his attitude and his ululation were intended to suggest a bear, but, unfortunately for his make-belief, instead of entering his friends' house he had mistakenly selected the one next door, where a conference of serious females was taking place in connection with some reform movement or other. The spectacle of an elderly, growling clergyman entering on all-fours created an immense sensation, which was increased when the embarrassed Mr. Dodgson suddenly rose to his feet and, without attempting any explanation, fled from the house with a celerity considerably more equine than ursine.

To help his rather faulty memory with regard to dates, he devised an elaborate system of mnemonics which he circulated among his friends. Another of his ingenious inventions to assist the memory was the "Nyctograph," a device to help him make notes in the dark. He was a poor sleeper, and new ideas would often occur to him in the night, during periods of wakefulness. At first he tried recording them on oblong slips of cardboard, but the results, more often than not, were illegible. So he invented his rather complicated "Nyctograph," which consisted of a series of squares cut out of cardboard on the edges of which he could write, using an alphabet of which each letter was formed with lines and dots. The system proved too intricate for various friends who tried it, on his recommendation; but apparently it worked very well with him.

The attraction which stage children had for Lewis Carroll led to a funny incident in connection with a visit he paid to the Princess's Theatre during the run of "Two Little Vagabonds", a play which pleased

E

him exceedingly. The occurrence is thus described in his diary:

"*December* 17th, 1895. I have given books to Kate Tyndall and Sydney Farebrother, and have heard from them, and find I was entirely mistaken in taking them for children. Both are married women!"

Two other ladies who were among the more intimate child friends of Lewis Carroll are Mrs. Alice Collett and Mrs. Norah MacFarlan. Among the letters I received after my Centenary talk on the "wireless" on January 27, 1932, those sent by these ladies are particularly interesting, as indicating the methods employed by Mr. Carroll to form and consolidate his innocent friendships. Mrs. Collett writes:

"My father had been a student of Christ Church, and had known Mr. Dodgson. When travelling with my mother and myself, a small girl of about five, he caught sight of Mr. Dodgson at a station, and, to our great delight, the author of 'Alice in Wonderland' joined us. It was generally a tedious journey for children to where we went every holiday, but this journey was entrancing.

"It was Lewis Carroll in his happiest mood, not Mr. Dodgson, who took me on his knee and told me stories and drew pictures for me, and the greatest thrill of all was just before he left us, when he produced a minute pair of scissors, about the size of his thumb-nail, and cut off a tiny lock of my hair, which he said he would put in a locket and always keep. I had the luck to be called Alice and to have a quantity of fair hair like his Alice, hence his interest."

Mrs. MacFarlan was little Norah Woodhouse when she first met the author of "Alice," in the following circumstances:

"Mother took a house at Eastbourne when we were children, and on the last day of our stay there, everything being packed up, we were allowed to go to the beach for a last paddle. I walked along a breakwater, fell in, and was soaked to the skin! I scrambled out, and was making my way along the beach, dripping, when I came across my sister Mabel, sitting by a strange, elderly gentleman, who was making a pencil sketch of her in his note-book, and stopped to greet her. Mr. Dodgson, for it was he, looked me gravely up and down, and then tore a corner of blotting paper from his note-book and said, "May I offer you this to blot yourself up?""

CHAPTER VII

THE REMINISCENCES OF ISA BOWMAN—LEWIS
CARROLL'S FOIBLES AND FANCIES—SHOCKED BY
"TA-RA-RA-BOOM-DE-AY"—HIS LOVE FOR THE
THEATRE.

AS a result of the lack of sympathy, in public,
between Lewis Carroll and Charles Dodgson,
it is not too much to say that the personality of
the former is less familiar than that of any great
Briton since Shakespeare, an obscurity of which
Mr. Dodgson, and possibly his family, too, might
approve; but which, I submit, is distinctly unfair
to Mr. Carroll and to the millions he has entertained and instructed.

I have already given a few details which may
compensate in a small measure for this omission,
as indicated in the reminiscences of some of his
juvenile friends who are now my adult friends.
From their more elaborated accounts, and in particular that of Mrs. Isa Barclay (formerly Miss
Isa Bowman) it is possible to draw the following
pen portrait of the gentle droll and his environment:

A slim, good-looking man of more than medium
height, his clean-shaven face was so unwrinkled
that it was difficult to tell his age, despite his
silver-grey hair which grew thickly all over his

ISA BOWMAN
(At the age of nine)

head and which he wore rather longer than is customary. His features were rather womanish and did not reflect his masculine strength of character, which amounted to obstinacy, and when he shook hands people were surprised by the vigour of his grip. His deep blue eyes invariably had a kindly twinkle in them, and he had rather a queer, jerky walk, which Miss Bowman attributes to him being slightly affected with that defect known as "housemaid's knee." This, and his occasional proneness to stammering, made him feel embarrassed in the presence of grown-ups with whom he was not well acquainted.

Sometimes in the middle of an animated conversation, and without any apparent cause, he would suddenly commence to stutter so much that it was difficult to understand him. Though he would often joke about this misfortune, with a kind of whimsical wonder at it, he strove hard to cure it, and to that end used to read aloud a scene from one of Shakespeare's plays every day.

In the company of grown-ups he was often almost old-maidishly prim, but with children this reserve would vanish completely, though it only required a slightly-disconcerting incident to bring the cloak of shyness back again. His fame, after the success of the "Alice" books, embarrassed him exceedingly, and to strangers who approached him for autographs he would invariably represent that Lewis Carroll, the author, and Charles Lutwidge

Dodgson, the professor, were two different persons, and the former could not be traced in Oxford.

His rooms, in the corner of Tom Quad, were approached through a heavy black door, on which was painted the inscription, "The Rev. C. L. Dodgson." This led to a short passage at the end of which a glass-panelled door opened on to his large and cheerful study. All round the walls were bookcases, and under them were low cupboards full of mechanical toys, puzzles, and other treasures calculated to amuse any young visitors. Among them were many musical boxes, the tunes for which were evolved from perforated cardboard discs, all carefully catalogued by their owner.

Opposite the window recess, with its cushioned seat, was the large fireplace, decorated with red tiles illustrating "The Hunting of the Snark." The framed photographs of little girl friends, taken by himself, were displayed here and there, but none of boys or babies, whom he only tolerated for their sisters' sakes.

In a large wardrobe was a stock of fancy costumes in which he loved to attire his little guests when they came to tea with him. Afterwards he would photograph them. The general arrangements of the room reflected the methodical and practical mind of Mr. Dodgson, rather than the absent-mindedness and whimsicality of Mr. Carroll, and there was nothing of the traditional untidiness of the literary man about them. His papers were so neatly and systematically arranged that he could put his hand on any particular document at a moment's notice, and he even numbered his correspondence. He loved receiving letters as well as writing them, and the last, which arrived the day before his death, raised the total to more than 98,000.

As a concession to the Carroll side of him, his manuscripts and letters were nearly always written in violet ink, and he invariably worked at them standing up at his desk.

Conversely, it is appropriate to assume that the educational and technical works he compiled under his real name were written in the hunched attitude impelled by occupancy of a chair, and inscribed in the customary funereal hue, but on this point I have no evidence. [1]

Whenever he travelled on a long railway journey his bag would be filled with ingenious mechanical toys and puzzles, mostly of his own invention, to amuse any nice little girl who might chance to be travelling in the same compartment. When this happened, the Dodgson stiffness was soon exchanged for the Carroll geniality, which was such that the adults in the compartment would also be invited to join in the fun. A speciality of his was a set of draughts and another of halma, in which the pieces could not overbalance or wobble, because they fitted into little holes in the board.

[1] Developing the same argument, it seems likely that the "Sylvie and Bruno" books, in which Carroll and Dodgson competed for predominance, were written partly in violet ink and partly in black, with one collaborator sitting and the other standing! But as this may seem rather a nonsensical assumption to some serious-minded people, I have rigorously relegated it to a footnote.

His personal eccentricities were many. At all seasons of the year he wore black cotton gloves, and nothing would induce him to wear an overcoat, or to change his attire once he had dressed for the day; so that he never "dressed for dinner," no matter whose invitation he might accept. Neither would he have a proper lunch—a glass of sherry and a biscuit or slice of melon usually sufficing.

Miss Isa Bowman's first meeting with Lewis Carroll was at the Prince of Wales Theatre, London, during a rehearsal of the stage version of "Alice in Wonderland"—a charming operetta, with music by Walter Slaughter, which opened at that theatre for a season of matinées during the Christmas of 1886. The part of Alice was played by little Phoebe Carlo, and that of the Mad Hatter by Sidney Harcourt.

Miss Nellie Bowman, then a tiny mite of seven, was taken by her mother to see the rehearsal, her elder sister, Isa, being in the play. Lewis Carroll watched the proceedings from the back of the auditorium, but came on the stage afterwards and talked to the players and their friends. He took an immediate fancy to the Bowman children, and after gravely asking their mother for the honour of an introduction soon made such friends with them that a special little part, that of a baby oyster, was written into the play for the younger sister. At the revival of the operetta at the Globe Theatre, two years later, Isa Bowman played the title role.

The musical director was Mr. (now Sir) Edward German, who in a letter to the writer of this biography recalls the fact that "the principals, chorus and orchestra seemed like a large family —so happy was everyone." Also that "Isa Bowman was Alice (and what a sweet little Alice she made!)"

Miss Irene Vanbrugh, then a girl of sixteen, made her London stage debut in the same production in the roles of the Knave of Hearts and the White Queen, the engagement being procured for her by Lewis Carroll himself, who was a friend of her father, the Reverend Prebendary Barnes. She tells me that the author of "Alice" made himself so entertaining to the children during rehearsal, with his stories and his fun, that more than once he was politely requested to leave the the theatre by the worried stage manager.

For several years in succession little Miss Bowman spent the summer holidays with Lewis Carroll and his housekeeper, Mrs. Dyer, at 7, Lushington Road, Eastbourne, and other vacations at Oxford (when not acting), where she stopped with the wife of one of his married colleagues.

"Uncle Charles," as the Bowman sisters always called their distinguished friend, engaged teachers for the little girl on various subjects, including the well-known Professor Beckwith of the old Westminster Aquarium to give her swimming lessons, a Swedish lady to teach her singing, and a Dutch one to instruct her in languages, at which she confesses she was a very indifferent pupil. He, himself, instructed her in geography (with the aid of jig-saw puzzles), arithmetic, Euclid and Biblical knowledge. The Scripture lessons were in the form of readings from the Bible, followed by explanations, after which she had to write out her own account of what she had heard, in the form of a little story.

"These lessons continued for years," says Miss Bowman, "and when my mother took me to America, where I played children's parts in Shakespearean repertoire, he sent them by post. For every day in the week, except Sunday, he arranged a schedule of lessons, supposed to last for about three hours, and these were faithfully adhered to—not altogether on account of any love of knowledge on my part, I fear."

Those were the days, many years before the advent of motion pictures, when motionless ones, in the form of panoramas, were popular. A few days before Miss Bowman left for America Mr. Dodgson took her to see the panorama of Niagara Falls, which was being exhibited at a hall in Regent Street, with the idea of giving her some practical instruction about the real Niagara, which she expected to see during her American visit.

As was the usual thing at these exhibitions, the immediate foreground, railed off from the public, consisted of grassy slopes and rocks, and to make the illusion of reality still more complete, a few waxen figures of tourists were grouped here and there.

Relates Miss Bowman:

"Uncle Charles was so impressed by the realistic model of a little dog which, with out-sticking tail and gaping mouth, appeared to be gazing with astonishment at the Falls that, in a moment the academic Dodgson, intent on geographical instruction, became effaced by the whimsical Carroll, who began relating to me a wonderful story about the dog which, he said, was really alive but trained to stand motionless for hours.

"'If you watch him ever so carefully,' he declared, 'you will see his tail move slightly.'

"'I do! I do!' I cried excitedly, and I really thought I did. Thus encouraged, Mr. Carroll added other absurd details about the dog, how, if we waited long enough, we would see an attendant bring him a bone, how he was allowed so many hours off each day when his brother, who unfortunately was rather restless, would take his place, and how this badly-behaved animal on one occasion jumped right out of the panorama among the onlookers, attracted by the sight of a little girl's sandwich, and so on. Suddenly he began to stammer and looking round in some alarm I saw that a dozen grown-ups and children had gathered around and were listening with every appearance of amused interest. And it was not Mr. Carroll, but a very confused Mr. Dodgson who took me by the hand and led me quickly from the scene.

"I enjoyed everything at Eastbourne except the meals. Uncle never seemed to consider that children required anything more substantial to eat than the frugal fare that satisfied him. With the exception of 'Ginger Snaps,' of which he was very fond, sweets and pastries and other delicacies dear to the childish heart were taboo, as harmful to me; although on occasions, when we used to walk up Beachy Head I was allowed a rock cake, as a special treat, when we reached the top. A favourite dish of his at lunch and dinner was a water melon with ginger or sugar, and often he would eat nothing else. Breakfast was equally meagre, and had it not been for surreptitious gifts of fruit and cake from Mrs. Dyer I should often have felt very hungry.

Incidentally, a queer characteristic of Mr. Dodgson was to take his own flask of sherry with him, whenever he lunched or dined away from home.

"His favourite colours were pink and grey, but he loathed scarlet, and was horrified when my mother dressed me in a scarlet frock. He also thought children should wear 'sensible' boots, and, much to my disgust, used to have clumsy, square-toed boots and shoes specially made for me by Dowie and Marshall when that firm had a shop[1] opposite Charing Cross Station, next to the Golden Cross Hotel.

"One of his many foibles was the making of tea, which he was often allowed to do when at the houses of his friends. After the tea had been made he would walk about the room, gravely swinging the tea-pot from side to side, to make its contents draw. At these outside tea-parties he would often make me feel embarrassed by exhibiting whatever talent I had for acting among his friends.

"'You can't make her smile,' he would say, 'just try!' As the result of this, and his friends' endeavours to test his boast, only made me more shy than ever, naturally I did not smile, whereupon he would declare, 'You see she is a real actress, with wonderful control over her features.' All the time he was, of course, laughing at me.

"He took my real acting very seriously, and when I was engaged for the part of the little Duke of York in "Richard the Third," with Richard Mansfield, the great American tragedian, at the old Globe Theatre, London, he seemed as proud of the honour as myself. But he could be a very severe critic. I remember calling upon him the day after the opening performance, and proudly showing him the references concerning myself which were in various London papers.

"'All very well,' he replied, 'but why do you pronounce "thank" as "thenk" when it is customary to spell it t-h-a-n-k?'

"He was most particular about pronunciation, and thinking of this made me feel like crying with sympathy for him, on the only occasion I heard him preach and witnessed his attempts to control his stuttering tongue.

[1] Now pulled down.

"He was a religious man in the best sense of the word; but though we had prayers every morning, his religion was never obtrusive. I remember being puzzled as to how to commence my childish prayers and asking his advice.

" 'If you always address God in your prayers as "My Dear Father in Heaven,' " he answered, 'you will find it will help you so much that you will never be at a loss for words to continue.'

"He was the purest-minded and cleanest living of men, intolerant of anything in the slightest degree coarse, and abominating a lie with an intensity which, in these days, would probably be regarded by most people as old-fashioned. He even objected against exaggerations of speech,[1] although the fact that he indulged in such exaggerations himself, in his writings and in his chaff, does not altogether absolve him from the gentle art of leg-pulling.[2] As is pretty generally known, he preferred children with straight hair. When I complained that my hair was becoming as straight as pokers he gravely pointed out that such a thing was impossible and drew a sketch of a child with pokers sticking out of her head to prove it.

"Sometimes, I fear, I used to shock him considerably. On one occasion he was charmed by hearing a small friend of mine, Florence Jackson (now a well-known actress in Shaw repertoire, etc.), sing 'The Holy City,' and when we returned to his rooms spoke with such appreciation of her beautiful voice that I began to feel a wee bit jealous and, in a spirit of naughtiness, said, 'I can sing too, Uncle—listen!' And, forthwith, I gave him a rendering of 'Ta-ra-ra-boom-de-ay!' which was then all the vogue, and accompanied it with a little dance.

"He stopped me before I could get to the second verse, and was so scandalised that I almost felt as though

[1] According to a letter written by the Rt. Rev. Edward Lee Hicks, a former Bishop of Lincoln, who was an undergraduate at Oxford when "Alice in Wonderland" was first written and well-acquainted with its author, the latter was the originator of that rather well-known joke, beloved of stage comedians, about a certain man who possessed such enormous feet that he had to put his trousers on over his head.

[2] Surely this is merely one more illustration of the difference in viewpoint between Mr. Dodgson and Mr. Carroll?

I had really done something dreadful. He used to say, 'No really good dancer, who is an artist, should ever raise her foot more than a few inches from the ground,' and he considered Kate Vaughan, whose dancing in long billowy skirts was of this order, to be the cleverest and most exquisite dancer in the world. He also had a very great appreciation for the work of such different lights of the entertainment world as Henry Irving, Ellen Terry and Albert Chevalier.

"He could not tolerate the idea of a man in petticoats, and on one occasion, when he went to see Nellie and Maggie in "The Water Babies,"[1] he walked out of the theatre when the comedian, Malcolm Scott, entered, dressed as a woman.

"On my return from America (when I was just fourteen) he was delighted when Ellen Terry offered to coach me in Shakespeare. He wrote me some lovely letters from Hatfield House, when I was playing the part of the little Duke of York, in one of which he said that as he was friendly with real Dukes he doubted very much whether he ought to know imitation ones.

"He really had a remarkable love for the theatre and for music, and at Eastbourne would spend many an afternoon at the Devonshire Park Concert Hall, listening to the splendid concerts for which it was noted. Sometimes they were so 'classical' that I must confess I was often very bored. Noticing that a number of old ladies made a practice of knitting, or doing some kind of fancy work at these functions, I thought I would pass away the time by doing the same; so one afternoon I produced some crochet and commenced to work upon it. After a time, he noticed what I was doing, and despite my excuse that I was only following the example of my elders, became exceedingly annoyed.

"'Do you not realise, my child,' he said, severely, 'that the artistes who are entertaining us this afternoon have probably spent a lifetime in perfecting themselves at their art? To show such public indifference to their efforts is to insult them. Never let me see you do this again!'

[1] Not to be confounded with Kingsley's "Water Babies," in the stage version of which Nellie Bowman played for three years in succession at the Garrick Theatre, London.

"Other things I remember about Mr. Dodgson were his high-pitched voice, the fact that I never saw him smoke, or heard of him smoking, his liking for backgammon, which we often used to play together, his remarkable skill in tying parcels, his vast collection of stylo pens and pencil sharpeners, which seemed to have a peculiar fascination for him—he had them in all sizes and colours—the large number of trunks which accompanied him whenever he left home for any considerable period, the fact that he always trimmed his nails with a clipper and never used scissors, and his invariable practice of ordering his notepaper to be made in five different sizes, ranging from a mere slip to a page much larger than usual. He was so precise that before he commenced a letter he would determine exactly what its length should be, and then fill up the whole of the sheet on both sides. 'Let me see,' he would say, 'For this letter I will use number three size, that should meet the case exactly.'

"And it always did."

While on the subject of Lewis Carroll's letters it is appropriate to remark that with the exception of Horace Walpole and William Cowper he appears to have been a more voluminous letter writer than any prominent British literary man of any period—even of the eighteenth century, when letter writing was practised as an art. And, like the two writers mentioned, he frequently revealed in intimate epistles, never intended for publication, his inmost thoughts.

CHAPTER VIII

THE LETTERS TO ELLEN TERRY—A SCHEME FOR TRAINING STAGE NOVITIATES—"THE JABBER-WOCK" AND THE TICHBORNE TRIAL.

UNDOUBTEDLY Lewis Carroll's greatest adult theatrical friend was Ellen Terry, whom he first saw in 1856, when, at the age of eight, she charmed him with her performance as the child Mamilius in "The Winter's Tale," with Charles Kean. A few years later he met her, and thus began a friendship with the Terry family which lasted till the day of his death.

Through the kindness of Miss Edith Craig, in permitting me to examine many of the letters which the author of "Alice in Wonderland" wrote to her distinguished mother from Christ Church, Oxford, I am privileged to throw an interesting light on this friendship by reproducing extracts from them. They are worthy as well as whimsical letters, which reflect the great kindness of heart possessed alike by their writer and their recipient.

One of the most interesting of them, written on April 26th, 1894, deplores the fact that minor players are afforded no opportunity of improving themselves in their art, during the hours of mono-tonous waiting, by watching the acting of the

"GEORGIE" AND CARROLL DODGSON, GRAND-NIECES OF LEWIS CARROLL
(*From two separate photographs by Vivian*)

principals, or of seeing any of the play except when they themselves are on the stage.

"I think the loss of such splendid opportunity for learning what good acting is like, is very great," says the letter, "and I am writing in the interest of the whole profession—even of the *leaders*, for *their* acting is to a great extent *lost* if they have not got good acting in the minor parts to support them."

After reminding Miss Terry of their old friendship, which he hopes will persuade her to hear "these very crude ideas of an amateur," he suggests a plan by which "as many supers and minor players as could stand in the wings without being in the way" should be allowed to see the play from this coign of vantage, the privilege to be extended to everybody in turn.

"My idea, then, if I were a manager, would be this: I would examine the wings, and see how many people could stand there, without being in the way, and be able to see the play. Suppose I found room for three on each side: then there might always be six watching.

"Then I would make strict rules as to who the six should be; I would arrange so that all the minor performers and supers should have the privilege in turn: also so that those who were watching should *not* be those who would be wanted immediately to go on (e.g., a super only wanted in Act III might safely be watching in Act II). And I would arrange so that, as far as possible, every one should witness (say in the course of a week or fortnight) the whole play bit by bit.

"Such a system would cost some trouble, no doubt. But surely *that* ought not to be a bar to it? It would, I think, do much to brighten the monotonous hours of waiting for all these supers, etc., and it would do much to help them in training themselves for future work,

F

and would thus be for the advantage of the leaders and of the public alike.

"Perhaps you have thought of all this already, and have found such a plan to be (from causes unknown to me) impossible: but if you *haven't*, *do* give it some consideration, and, if possible, get Mr. Irving also to consider whether some change cannot be made (if only as an experiment) in the present system."

Whether the scheme proposed was ever put into effect by Irving I do not know, but from my own knowledge of the stage I feel sure that its practicality was and is obviated by the facts that the minor players in a big production usually appear in a variety of meagre impersonations, the dressing for which allows no hours of monotonous waiting, and that a large proportion of them, particularly in Shakespearean repertoire, so far from being tyros, are "old troupers," who have probably had as much experience as any of the principals, although lacking either the talent or the influence necessary for advancement. It is well known that Irving regularly employed a large number of supers of this type.

A much earlier letter, dated April 14th, 1881, contains several fine and original reflections:

"I have not lived all these years without being able fully to sympathise with you in the wretchedness of being 'tired.' It is the general cry of human life, I think, from the cradle to the grave. 'So tired, so tired, my heart and I!' I wonder if the life of a day is *meant* to symbolise the life of three-score years and ten. It is so startlingly like it: the fresh vigour of the first hour or so: and the strength of noonday work: and the

'tiredness' that begins to creep on through the afternoon: and last (I suppose) the contented weariness of
the old man, when he 'wraps the drapery of his couch
about him and lies down to pleasant dreams'—well, the
'afternoon' is pleasant enough after all, 'tired' as one
sometimes is. May you find it so when you come to it—
but you are in all the blaze of noonday just now.

"Please always excuse yourself from writing to me
when you don't feel up to it."

Another interesting letter, dated November 13th,
1890, refers to Miss Terry's kindness in giving
elocution lessons to little Isa Bowman, when the
most the writer expected was that the great actress
would provide him with the names and addresses
of a few good teachers.

"What *is* one to do with a friend who does
about a hundred times more than you ask her to
do?" he enquires, and then declares that Miss
Terry must have discovered that "one of the deep
secrets of life is that all that is really worth doing
is what we do for others."

A fourth letter, written on June 7th, 1894,
expresses gratitude to Miss Terry and Henry
Irving for their kindness to a young friend, "whose
need it is to earn money," and whimsically deplores
the shortness of the interview on the occasion of
a recent visit when he introduced another youthful
friend to Miss Terry behind the scenes.

"That isn't at all the sort of interview I like best
with old friends," continues the letter, "tête-à-têtes are
what I like best. Now that I have entered on the stage
of being 'a lean and slippered pantaloon,' and no
longer dread the frown of Mrs. Grundy, I have taken to

giving tête-à-tête dinner parties—the guest being, in most cases, a lady of age varying from 12 to 67 (the maximum I have yet had); and they are *very* pleasant. If you were staying in Oxford, I really think (however incredible it might sound) that I should have the 'cheek' to ask you to come and dine so!"

Another letter, written about the same period, is unconsciously humorous in its recommendation of a stage-struck and penurious young friend who, "with a little more experience and a little more courage to throw herself into a part and let it carry her away, should be useful in any part where a *lady* is needed."

In the same letter, Lewis Carroll entreats Miss Terry to give a line or two to "a dear *good* child, that little friend of mine, Clara Earle, whom you enriched with a kiss on Friday," and suggests that she ought to have, at the Lyceum, "one who is, I verily believe, the cleverest child now on the stage, my sweet little friend Empsie Bowman. Do go and see her in 'The Little Squire,' at the Lyric."

Miss Bowman's eldest sister, Isa, played an important part in the same piece, concerning which she tells me: 'In some ways 'Uncle' was curiously narrow. He hated me playing the wicked girl in 'The Wicked Squire,' and for the time it ran was never quite so nice to me; he loved Empsie in the same play."

Through the kindness of the Scott-Gatty family, I have also had the privilege of perusing some of the interesting letters written by Lewis Carroll to

Mrs. Alfred Gatty and her daughter, now Mrs. Eden.

In a letter, dated February 24th, 1870, he expresses his views on publicity, thus:

"As to you telling friends my name, though I don't want it published in *print*, I have no objection to your giving any private information you choose. Members of the general public, writing to you as strangers to ask the question, do not seem to me to have any claim to such communication."

In the same letter he suggests that Mrs. Gatty might like to see the "Gazette," written for the amusement of Mr. Synge and his friends and speaks of the clever metrical version of "Kenilworth," made by this gentleman, also of having met Miss Thackeray "and the little boy, Thackeray, godson of W.M.T." (William Makepeace Thackeray) at the novelist's house.

The Mr. Synge in question was William Webb Follett Synge, a friend of Thackeray, who was born in 1826, died in 1891, and was a diplomatist and author, who entered the Foreign Office in 1846, contributed to "Punch" and "Blackwood's Magazine" and wrote some verses for children. The "Gazette" seems to have been an amateur journal of a more ambitious and more mature kind than the "Rectory Umbrella," and apparently, there was only one issue of it. Its full title was the "Guildford Gazette Extraordinary," though it was printed at Oxford, in 1870. It contained, among other matter, verses by Lewis Carroll relating to the opening of a new theatre at Guildford. The only known copy now in existence is in the possession of Mr. Parrish, of Philadelphia.

A letter written to Miss Gatty on February 15th, 1872, thus refers to a proposal to publish "Jabberwocky" by itself, with music:

> "I hope your brother has largely abridged the poem, as I should think that the whole, if sung to a slow air, would remind one more of the Tichborne trial than of any other form of entertainment now popular."

Finally I have a letter, written to my friend, Mr. J. W. Gordon, K.C., on October 27th, 1897, which, though very brief, is particularly interesting to me, for the reason that it supports my belief that Messrs. Carroll and Dodgson were different personalities inhabiting one physical body. The letter, in question, is entirely a Dodgson letter, not only in substance but in its curt and uncordial style.

Mr. Gordon, mathematician as well as barrister, had written to Mr. Dodgson, pointing out that the latter's claim to have established a new rule of division in a set of mathematical tables published in "Nature" could not be substantiated, as he (Mr. Gordon) had prepared a set of similar mathematical tables two years earlier, and had published an explanatory pamphlet concerning them. He enclosed a copy of the set of tables and another of the pamphlet and modestly explained:

> "I have taken the liberty of mentioning this coincidence mainly because I imagine it will amuse you, and

that so far as I am aware of any "Arrière pensée" at all it is only that I am covetous of an opportunity of submitting my work to a mathematician for whose genius I have long felt profound respect, in circumstances which promise me the advantage of his momentary interest in my results."

In reply, Mr. Dodgson indicated that he would be glad to keep the pamphlet but intended to return the tables:

"As they are absolutely wasted on me; I am much too busy with other subjects to have any chance at all, at my time of life, of ever taking to mathematical work again."

It is interesting to note that the letters from which I have taken these various extracts were all written in black ink, which suggests that the partiality of their writer for ink of a violet hue, to which several of his friends have borne witness, must have been confined to his manuscripts.

CHAPTER IX

LEWIS CARROLL AND LOVE—HIS DISLIKE OF
BABIES—HIS JEALOUSY—WHY HE NEVER MARRIED
—HIS TALENT AS AN ART AND DRAMATIC CRITIC
—THE PASSING OF CHARLES LUTWIDGE DODGSON.

TO the characteristics of Lewis Carroll enumerated in the preceding chapters should be
added his abomination of babies, his pronounced
predilection for the life of a bachelor, and his
jealousy. It is comforting to be able to mention
these weaknesses (if the first *is* a weakness in a *man !*)
in a nature which otherwise might seem to be
almost too idealistic to be entirely credible.

Of his anti-baby bias he has left a record in a
letter to his friend, Dr. C. H. O. Daniel, Provost
of Worcester College, Oxford, indefatigable amateur author and publisher, who periodically favoured
his friends with productions from his private press
and solicited their contributions to the same. To
celebrate the second birthday of his baby daughter,
Rachel, he invited some of his friends to contribute
each a poem on the interesting event to a collection
of such tributes which he proposed to publish under
the title of "Garland of Rachel." Lewis Carroll's
reply to the invitation was dated November 23rd,
1880, and ran as follows:

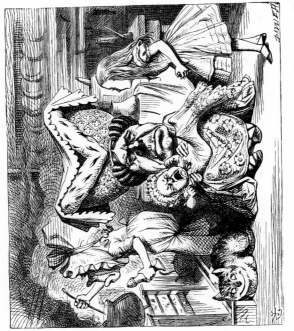

Tenniel's Drawing of the Duchess, from "Alice in Wonderland"

"My dear Daniel,

"As to the typical human Baby, what hope is there? The subject is exhausted, I fear—(parenthetically, I hate babies, but that is irrelevant). And I suppose you want something serious—not *this* style, for instance:

> "Oh pudgy, podgy pup!
> Why *did* they wake you up?
> Those crude nocturnal yells
> Are *not* like silver bells:
> Nor ever would recall
> Sweet Music's 'dying fall.'
> They rather bring to mind
> The bitter winter wind
> Through keyholes shrieking shrilly
> When nights are dark and chilly:
> Or like some dire duet,
> Or quarrelsome quartette,
> Of cats who chant their joys
> With execrable noise,
> And murder Time and Tune
> To vex the patient Moon!"

It is, perhaps, unnecessary to add that Dr. Daniel did *not* include this libellous lyric in his poetic "bouquet."

With regard to the charge of jealousy against the subject of this biography, I have been assured of its justification by several of those who were best calculated to form a first-hand opinion. He could not bear to hear of his former child friends marrying, even though he had lost all interest in their personal friendship, and on occasion he exhibited an almost childish jealousy against the affection of their parents.

And yet, it is certain that he never had a love affair, or even any flirtations, though he must have known many beautiful and charming young women whose affection he had gained as children. I am assured by Major Dodgson and Miss F. Menella Dodgson that in all the very revealing matter discovered in his numerous diaries there is not the slightest suggestion that he either felt or inspired any pangs of the tender passion, and the testimony of various friends with whom he occasionally discussed intimate and personal questions, and whom I have interviewed, is to the same effect.

His interest in his child friends usually ceased when they were about fourteen and when, despite this, any of them sought to keep the flame of friendship alive he much preferred to exchange correspondence with them on the subject of their spiritual welfare than to renew their former intimacy.

One of the very few exceptions was Ellen Terry, whom he first met as a child actress, and who remained his friend until his death. His letters to her and certain entries in his diary show that he admired her greatly; but that this feeling was entirely prompted by her acting talent and her fine qualities of heart and mind may be gathered from the fact that the most ardent tribute to her to be found in his diaries is concerned with an entry in which he thus comments upon the duties of a companion engaged by Miss Terry to read to her and to brush her hair: "I can imagine no more delightful occupation than brushing Ellen Terry's hair!" And in none of the letters which I have been privileged to examine is she addressed by any term more endearing than, "My Dear Miss Ellen Terry," or "My Dear Old Friend," while they are all signed either "Always Yours Affectionately," or "Always Yours Sincerely."

What Miss Edith Craig has told me with reference to the friendship between Lewis Carroll and her distinguished mother endorses the views expressed above, and proves the existence of yet another original trait in the nature of this most original man—he was one of the very few men—possibly the only one—who had known Ellen Terry in her prime without falling in love with her!

Having met the great actress thrice myself I am able to give first-hand testimony that, even at the age of seventy, her personal fascination was extraordinary.

One rumour with regard to a romantic attachment on the part of the subject of this biography being thus obliterated, let us utterly disprove another. The story published in a London daily newspaper in January, 1932, to the effect that Lewis Carroll had been in love with Violet Liddell, and that parental opposition to an engagement between them caused her to die of a broken heart at the age of nineteen, and prompted him to irrevocable bachelorship, is entirely without foundation. It is best refuted by epitomising the history of the five Liddell sisters.

In the present year (1932), Alice, now Mrs. Hargreaves, and Rhoda, the youngest, are still alive. Violet Liddell died, an old lady, in December, 1927, and is hardly mentioned in the diaries; Lorina married Mr. Skene in 1874 and died in 1930, and Edith, born January 23rd, 1854, died from the effect of measles in 1876, and was buried outside the south-east corner of Oxford Cathedral. She was engaged to Mr. Aubrey Harcourt, who died a bachelor some years afterwards.

It has been suggested that the reason why Lewis Carroll was proof against love was because he was "incapable of marriage." This I do not believe. I feel sure that the real reason was because he was one of those super-sensitive and over-refined people to whom the very idea of physical familiarity was abhorrent. Nearly everyone has met natures so constituted, and it is a condition which undoubtedly provides the answer as to why so many charming and healthy women develop into old maids and others take the veil.

Even in his serious love poems (written between 1860 and 1862) which constitute the greater part of the volume of his collected verse published under the title of one of them, "The Three Sunsets," love is always treated as spiritual development, and the loss of the unhappy man who rejects it in the two most tragic of these poems is emphasised as a spiritual loss and not as a physical or even a social and domestic one. And, almost without exception, his later poems which deal with the tender passion ridicule the subject unmercifully.

With Lewis Carroll, love was essentially a condition of the affections and not of the passions. Being half a child in heart himself, it was impossible for him to believe that personal love of one nature for another could exist, outside the family circle, in any purer form than that represented by the affection of a girl child. Obviously he was guided largely by his particular aesthetic tastes, but the fact remains. In a rhymed acrostic, written in 1878 for a small friend named Sarah Sinclair, he answers a question supposed to be asked by "fairy sprites," who are desirous of finding Love, by bidding them seek "in childhood's heart so pure and clear." And an interesting series of letters he wrote to a former child friend, Miss Mary Brown, who made repeated efforts to continue their friendship until his death, and was successful so far as correspondence was concerned, indicate that he deliberately discouraged personal friendship with grown girls he had known as children, in the conviction that such association could only injure the memory of the idealistic comradeship he had exchanged with them before they had acquired any adult worldliness or sophistication.

He first met Miss Brown when, as a child of seven, she attracted his sympathy by crying over a torn stocking on a seat at Whitby and the two became great friends during her stay there.

"I never saw him after that," Miss Brown informed the present writer, "yet, until his passing away we kept writing; if I did not write for a long time a puzzle would come, or something to remind me I had not done so."

The following extracts from his letters to this lady are particularly illuminating:

(*April 1st*, 1889): "Ours is a strange sort of friendship and we must be getting very unreal to each other by this time. It must be nearly twenty years since we met, and it is *very doubtful* if we should even recognise each other now! My memory of you, as a little girl who sat on my knee (a performance you may have totally forgotten by now) out on the cliffs at Whitby, and yours of me—well, of not quite such an old 'lean and slippered pantaloon' as I have now become! That our friendship should have survived *at all*, through all these years, is something wonderful; and whether it would stand the shock of meeting again—whether our characters have not become, by this time, hopelessly discordant, is an open question!"

(*December 26th*, 1889): "I have been putting off from day to day writing an answer to your letter of the 13th—not from indolence and not (most certainly) from want of love for you; how can I *help* loving one who has gone on loving me all these years, without one single meeting to revive her memory of me, since that long ago when she sat on my knee as a little girl?"

The rest of this letter is mainly concerned with enquiry and advice on spiritual matters, and contains valuable information as to the writer's religious views, with which I have dealt in another chapter.

How emphatic was Lewis Carroll's determination to maintain his bachelor freedom may be gathered from the following extract from a letter he wrote, at the age of fifty-two, to an old college friend:

"So you have been for twelve years a married man, while I am still a lonely old bachelor! And mean to

keep so for the matter of that. College life is by no
means an unmixed misery, though married life has, no
doubt, many charms to which I am a stranger."

If any proof were needed of the perfect sympathy
and understanding that existed between Lewis
Carroll and his little friends, it may be found in
the fact that they never extended to him that
natural propensity of most children for making
fun of their elders behind their backs.

Says Mr. Bert Coote, in recalling this fact:

"My sister and I were regular young imps, and nothing
delighted us more at parties than to give imitations of
some of our grown-up friends, while if we accompanied
one of them anywhere a giggling duet was sure to commence presently over some eccentricity, real or imagined,
which amused us. It must have been very embarrassing to our adult companion. But we never gave
imitations of Lewis Carroll, or shared any joke in which
he could not join—he was one of us, and never a grown-
up pretending to be a child in order to preach at us,
or otherwise instruct us. We saw nothing funny in his
eccentricities, perhaps he never was eccentric among
children, or may be he had the brain of a clever and
abnormal man with the heart of a normal child. I shall
never forget the morning he took my sister and I over
the Tower of London and how fascinated we were by the
stories he told us about it and its famous prisoners. I
suspect now that very few of them were based on strict,
historical fact, but that they would have charmed any
child there is no question. He was a born story-teller,
and if he had not been affected with a slight stutter in
the presence of grown-ups would have made a wonderful
actor, his sense of the theatre was extraordinary."

On this last point, Miss Nellie Bowman tells me
that he would offer the most helpful advice and

criticism as to the inflection and emphasis she and her sisters should give to the lines of their various parts, and he wrote them several letters to this effect.

In these days, when the theatre has been degraded by the misdirected energies of high-brow fanatics and unintellectual "intellectuals," who ignore its essential function of entertainment and persist in regarding it as a medium through which to impose upon an apathetic public their personal idiosyncrasies and "ologies," which are invariably allied with ugliness and gloom, the opinion of Lewis Carroll on its proper function is particularly interesting. Here it is, as recorded in a passage of his diary for June 22nd, 1853, in which he refers to an evening spent at the Princesses's Theatre, London:

"Then came the great play, "Henry VIII," the greatest theatrical treat I have ever had or expect to have. I had no idea that anything so superb as the scenery and dresses was ever to be seen on the stage. Kean was magnificent as Cardinal Wolsey, Mrs. Kean a worthy successor to Mrs. Siddons as Queen Catherine, and all the accessories, without exception, were good—but, oh that exquisite vision of Queen Catherine! I almost held my breath to watch, the illusion was perfect, and I felt as if in a dream the whole time it lasted. It was like a delicious reverie or most beautiful poetry. This is the true end and object of acting—to raise the mind above itself and out of its petty cares."

The modern "legitimate" stage has so far lost sight of this "true end and object" that it is no wonder its existence is imperilled by the musical extravaganza and the cinema, which with all their faults do at least seek to entertain, and thus do achieve something in the direction of "raising the mind out of its petty cares."

His last visit to the theatre was in 1897, a few weeks before his death, when he saw Barrie's "Little Minister" at the Haymarket Theatre, London:

"A beautiful play, beautifully acted, and one I would like to see again and again."

He particularly admired the acting of Miss Winifred Emery (Mrs. Cyril Maude) in this. There are many other entries in his diaries which indicate his lifelong love for the theatre and reveal a power for dramatic criticism which would probably have gained him high honours as a dramatic critic, had he become one professionally. Equally brillant are his art criticisms, particularly those in connection with the Royal Academy, which he made a point of attending regularly during the opening week, arriving as soon as the doors were open and departing by eleven to avoid the crowd. His knowledge of the painter's art, both of the modern schools and the mediæval, was profound, and when persuaded to talk on the subject he could do so most engrossingly.

An amusing art criticism, made in his diary during his Continental tour with Dr. Liddon in 1867, which I am permitted to quote, is the following:

"The amount of art lavished on the whole region of Potsdam is marvellous; some of the tops of the palaces

were like forests of statues, and they were all over the
gardens, set on pedestals. In fact, the two principals
of Berlin architecture appear to me to be these. On the
house-tops, wherever there is a convenient place, put
up the figure of a man; he is best placed standing on
one leg.   Wherever there is room on the ground, put
either a circular group of busts on pedestals, in consulta-
tion, all looking inwards—or else the colossal figure of
a man killing, about to kill, or having killed (the present
tense is preferred)a beast; a dragon is the correct thing,
but if that is beyond the artist, he may content himself
with a lion or a pig. The beast-killing principle has
been carried out everywhere with a relentless monotony,
which makes some parts of Berlin look like a fossil
slaughter-house."

On the other hand, although he enjoyed listening
to concerts, and could enthuse over an anthem or
a sentimental ballad; he had no real ear for
music, and was incapable of producing harmony
on any instrument that was not mechanically
controlled, and the musical criticisms in his diaries
are so puerile as to be almost comic.

Had it not been for a sudden and fatal attack
of influenza, while staying at his sister's house at
Guildford, Charles Lutwidge Dodgson would probably have lived to a green old age, for at the age
of sixty-five he was unusually virile, both physically
and mentally. With his retirement from his mathematical duties he had discarded much of the
Dodgson formality and aloofness, and had become
more wholly Carrollian than he had been at any
time during his long engagement at Christ Church.
Wearing a top hat and clerical frock coat, he
thought nothing of walking twenty miles over the

Surrey hills on a broiling July day, an experience which the nephew who sometimes accompanied him assures the biographer he, himself, found exhausting. Charles Lutwidge Dodgson died on January 14th, 1898, after a few days illness, at his sister's house, "The Chestnuts," Guildford, where for some twenty years it had been his custom to spend the Christmas and other holidays. He was buried in Guildford Old Cemetery, on the slopes of the "Hog's Back," where a plain white cross and a triple pediment "erected in loving memory by his brothers and sisters," bears the following inscription:

CHARLES LUTWIDGE DODGSON
(Lewis Carroll.)

Fell Asleep, January 14th, 1898

Age 65 years.

"Where I am there shall also my servant be."
"His servants shall serve him."

"Father, in thy gracious keeping
Leave we now thy servant sleeping."

A grave[1] as modest and unpretentious as the man himself. Over the head of the tomb droops a beautiful yew tree, whose branches shelter it lovingly from storms and heat, and whose trunk is entwined with little heart-shaped ivy leaves, just as the genius sleeping there attracted the hearts of little children a generation ago and his works will continue to do for all time.

[1] The Guildford Town Council have now taken over the upkeep of the grave in perpetuity "in token of Guildford's pride in remembrance."

For it is merely Charles Lutwidge Dodgson who died. Lewis Carroll is very much alive and, indeed, has never been more vital than he is to-day. In such anxious and troublous times as have jarred us since 1914, so entertaining and soothing a comforter has become indispensable, and the tribute to him as an "antidote" to the miseries of war in Mr. Sherrif's play, "Journey's End", is justified.

His quaint words, phrases, similes and paradoxes have become incorporated in the English language, and are probably employed by [preachers, politicians, pedagogues, playwrights and everyday people more frequently than those of any other writer of the last three hundred years. Some of them, including "Jam to-morrow and jam yesterday, but never jam to-day," . . . "Cabbages and Kings," . . . "As large as life and twice as natural," . . . "He only does it to annoy, because he knows it teases," and those indispensable words "chortle" and "burble" are as well known to the English-speaking nations as anything in Shakespeare.

It is almost impossible to read through a British or American newspaper without finding one or two "Carrollisms," and in times of political stress the characteristics of various more or less eminent statesmen are assured of being likened to those of "The Mad Hatter."

No wonder that an inspection of London's advertisements reveals the fact that Lewis Carroll has inspired more examples of poster art than any other half-a-dozen writers put together. On the morning I penned these lines I found that those handsome poster galleries—so thoughtfully provided by the beneficent authorities of London's Tube railways, to render the parade of their subterranean platforms a pleasure instead of a pilgrimage—displayed two such advertisements, one associating the "Duchess" with a popular brand of Hibernian stout and the other connecting the famous "Lobster Quadrille" with a well-known sauce.

A transference not from the sublime to the ridiculous, as some Carroll devotees will probably declare but from the sublime to the practical.

CHAPTER X

LEWIS CARROLL AND HIS RELIGION—HIS
UNORTHODOXY—HIS VIEWS ON SACRED SUBJECTS
IN THE THEATRE, ON HUMOUR IN THE PULPIT,
CASUISTRY, HEAVEN, HELL, AND TOTAL ABSTIN-
ENCE.

AS might be expected, Lewis Carroll's religion
was unorthodox, both in expression and in
practice. At the same time, it was also the religion
of C. L. Dodgson, for on matters of sacred belief
there was no question of dual personality or
divergent opinions. Each could say with his
great American contemporary, Oliver Wendell
Holmes: "All that I have seen teaches me to trust
the Creator for all I have not seen," which seems
to me to define the principles of Lewis Carroll's
religion exactly. He had no use for dogma, or for
man-made definitions which explained God so
completely that faith and trust were rendered
superfluous; religion with him was not a lesson
to be learned, but a responsibility to be undertaken
and enjoyed.

And so it was not principally on account of his
stammering that he never undertook regular clerical
duties and sought no advancement in the Church.
Graver reasons were his repugnance to the narrow-

ness of the Anglican outlook in the 'sixties which,
among other reprehensions, disapproved of any
connection between parsons and play-going, and
his inability to subscribe to the Thirty-Nine Articles.
This he admitted, in an intimate talk he had with
Miss Irene Vanbrugh and her sister Violet, while
walking with them one morning on Eastbourne
Front. On the same occasion he explained that
his idea of Paradise was not a single Heaven, but
a succession of celestial planes to which the souls of
the deserving would be translated according to the
merits of their lives on earth, to be again translated
to higher planes as they became spiritually developed
for such promotion. He also told the same ladies
that one of the greatest joys he expected to find
in Heaven would be the solution to problems of
mathematical infinity! A hope that may strike the
trivial and irreverent as trivial and irreverent.

Actually Lewis Carroll's religion was the most
important factor in his life, and no fanatic was ever
more sure of its indulgences and injunctions.
Sincerity and dignity were its keynotes, as is
evident from the preface to "Sylvie and Bruno
Concluded," in which he says:

"While freely admitting that the "Ritual" movement
was sorely needed, and that it has effected a vast im-
provement in our Church Services, which had become
dead and dry to the last degree, I hold that like many
other desirable movements, it has gone too far in the
opposite direction and has introduced many new dangers.
"For the Congregation this new movement involves the
danger of learning to think that the Services are done

for them; and their bodily *presence* is all that they need contribute. And, for the Clergy and Congregation alike, it involves the danger of regarding these elaborate Services as ends in *themselves*, and forgetting that they are simply *means*, and the very hollowest of mockeries, unless they bear fruit in our *lives*. . . . According to *my* experience, Clergymen of this school are *specially* apt to retail comic anecdotes, in which the most sacred names and words—sometimes actual texts from the Bible—are used as themes for jesting. Many such things are repeated as having been originally said by *children*, whose utter ignorance of evil must no doubt acquit *them*, in the sight of God, of all blame; but it must be otherwise for those who *consciously* use such innocent utterances as material for their unholy mirth."

His opinions with regard to the stage presentation of sacred incidents were equally inflexible, in illustration of which I quote an extract from an article he wrote for the " Theatre," for June, 1888, and another from a letter to Miss Helen Fielden, in 1881, which, though appearing at first glance to be contradictory, are entirely concordant:

"Places of worship when made the subject of stage representation are usually treated with perfect propriety: one must turn to the orgies of the Salvation Army or the ribaldry of the street preacher to realise how far religion can be vulgarised, and with what loathsome familiarity the holiest things can be insulted."

"Many thanks for your history of the 'Oberammergau Passion Play.' I am much interested in reading accounts of the play; and I thoroughly believe in the deep religious feeling with which the actors go through it; but would not like to see it myself. I am very fond of the theatre, but I had rather keep my ideas and recollections of it quite distinct from those about the Gospels."

At a juvenile performance he witnessed of " H.M.S. Pinafore " he even took strong exception

against children singing the lyric which refers to
the fact that the Captain "hardly ever sings a big
—big D——" and wondered how Gilbert could
write such "trash" and Sullivan could put music
to it! And, as Miss Isa Bowman has shown, he had
an irrevocable antipathy against men appearing on
the stage dressed as women. He could see no
humour in anything that even faintly savoured of
vulgarity, or in any serious topic treated lightly—or
what he imagined was lightly—in the pulpit, a
trait in his character which has perplexed many
excellent people, including the writer of a letter,
signed "Minnie Tollington," which was published
in "The Times" on December 24th, 1931, and
stated:

"My father, the late Bishop Boyd-Carpenter, delivered
the Bampton Lectures in Oxford in the year 1887.
Referring to the conflict between religion and science,
and the occasions when each blamed the other for unhappy differences of opinion, my father added, 'Why,
this is the old domestic quarrel in which each parent
says to the other: "Clearly this fault in our child is the
outcome of characteristics well known to belong to your
family."' An audible if suppressed titter ran through
the learned congregation. A letter of protest was sent,
of all people, by Lewis Carroll to my father deprecating
the introduction of any element of amusement into a
sermon. Homer nods. Did a sense of humour for
once fail the delightful author of 'Alice'? The letter
may be seen in Dr. Major's 'Life and Letters of the
Bishop,' p. 184."

His own sermons were models of logical sim-
plicity and seriousness—I have a copy of one of
them before me as I write—a child could have

understood them. His arguments were equally lucid and reasoned. Consider his ingenious refutation of the Casuist contention that to derive pleasure by giving pleasure to others is merely a refined kind of selfishness. Here it is, as expressed in a letter to Miss Ellen Terry, dated November 13th, 1890:

"The selfish man is he who would still do the thing, even if it harmed others, so long as it gave *him* pleasure; the unselfish man is he who would still do the thing, even if it gave him no pleasure, so long as it *pleased others*. But when both motives pull together, the unselfish man is still the unselfish man, even though his own pleasure *is* one of his motives. I am very sure that God takes real *pleasure* in seeing his children happy!"

Even more interesting are the revelations of Lewis Carroll's convictions with regard to the constituents of Right and Wrong and the savage doctrine of "Eternal Punishment," so beloved of the Victorian puritans; and a study of them suggests that he had considerably more belief in "original goodness" than in "original sin." What could be more lucid or logical than the following views, expressed in letters he wrote to Miss Mary Brown between 1880 and 1889?

"As to the words, 'This day shalt thou be with me in Paradise' and the words in the Apostles' Creed, 'He descended into Hell,' the usual interpretation is that both words refer to the 'place of departed spirits,' where, as we believe, the disembodied spirits await the time of resurrection, when they shall be clothed in their 'spiritual bodies' and shall appear before the judgment seat of Christ and so shall pass to Heaven or to

Hell. The parable of the rich man and Lazarus seems to teach us that even among the disembodied spirits *distinction* is made, some being in happiness and others in sorrow. The two separate portions of this world of spirits are called, in the Greek 'Paradise' (or 'Abraham's bosom') and 'hades.' This later words occurs in (here follow eleven Biblical references).

"In 1 Corinthians xv. 55, it is translated 'grave' and in the other instances 'hell,' which I think a misleading translation, being liable to be confused with the Greek word 'Gehenna' (which is also translated to 'hell'), the name of the place to which the wicked shall be sent *after* the resurrection. The word 'gehenna' occurs in twelve places (here follow references). That it refers to a place not reached till *after* the resurrection is clear from Matthew x. 28.

"So, in answer to your question, I say, in the first place, it is not the teaching of the Bible (though no doubt it is taught in many human writings, such as sermons and hymns) that *anyone* is sent either to Heaven or to Hell *immediately* after death. . . . I believe I am responsible to a *Personal Being* for what I do. I believe that Being to be *perfectly good* and I call that Perfect Being 'God.' Now put side by side with that the theory 'God will punish all persons *equally* who commit the same sin, though the temptations may have been, owing to difference of circumstances, irresistible by the one and easily resisted by the other.'

"I say this contradicts the perfect goodness of God. One of the two must be false. I hold to the first theory— namely, that God is perfectly good; and I deny the *second*. That is, I say God will not act thus. If you urge that such and such a text asserts it . . . I reply then either the Bible is not inspired, or the text is not genuine, or it is mistranslated.

"From the belief that God is perfectly good, I conclude, as necessary sequences, that He will take account of all circumstances in judging of any error of man, and that he will not punish except for *wilful* sin, where the sinner was free to choose between good or evil— that he will not punish for *ever* anyone who *desires* to repent.

"If anyone says it is certain the Bible teaches that once a man is in Hell, no matter how much he repent, there he will stay for ever, I reply that if I were certain the Bible taught that, I would give up the Bible. And if anyone urges then, that to be consistent, I ought to grant the possibility that the Devil himself might repent and be forgiven, I reply that I do grant it!"

From a later letter:

"I find it one of the many pleasures of old age (I think at 57 I may call myself an old man) to be allowed to enter into the inner lives and secret sorrows of child friends, now grown to be women, and to give them such comfort and advice as I can. It makes one very humble in view of one's own need of guidance and unfitness to guide, and very thankful to God for thus letting one work for him."

How unimportant Lewis Carroll considered the dogmas which distinguish the various Christian religions may be gathered by the picture he draws in "Sylvie and Bruno Concluded," of the three devoted ministers of religion who risk their lives in a plague-stricken village:

"gallant heroes as ever won the Victoria Cross. I am certain that no one of the three will ever leave the place merely to save his own life. There's the Curate: his wife is with him: they have no children. Then there's the Roman Catholic Priest. And there's the Wesleyan Minister. They go amongst their own flocks mostly; but I'm told that those who are dying like to have any of the three with them. How slight the barriers seem to be that part Christian from Christian, when one has to deal with the great Facts of Life and the reality of Death!"

Just as it was impossible for Lewis Carroll, as a logical human being, to subscribe to the unholy doctrine of eternal punishment, so his reason exposed to him the absurdity and futility of the puritan contention that total abstinence on the part of the moderate drinker must necessarily offer a good example to the drunkard. Consider this ingenious parable in reply to a total abstinence fanatic of this type, as quoted from the work I mentioned last:

"I was once a moderate sleeper and met a man who slept to excess. 'Give up this lying in bed,' I said, 'it will ruin your health.'

"'You go to bed, why shouldn't I?' he said.

"'Yes,' I said, 'but I know when to get up in the morning.'

"He turned away from me. 'You sleep in your way,' he said, 'let me sleep in mine. Be off!'

"I saw that to do any good with him I must forswear sleep. From that hour I have never been to bed!"

That Lewis Carroll practised what he preached cannot be doubted. I have conclusive evidence of many good deeds he did by stealth. One of them concerned his mysterious disappearance from his usual Christ Church haunts for two whole days. Later, it leaked out that for two days and two night, without any rest himself, he had nursed a poor, friendless man—a minor college servant—who had been stricken with typhoid fever in his lodgings in an obscure part of the city. And his generosity to the Great Ormonde Street Hospital and other hospitals for children is, of course, pretty well known. In this connection it will be appropriate to conclude the present chapter with a true anecdote, related to him by the matron of the hospital mentioned, which he used to declare was one of the most beautiful stories he had ever heard.

It appears that one of the patients, a little fellow aged six, *would* sleep with one arm outside the bed-clothes, despite all attempts to dissuade him. On being asked the reason, he explained that if Jesus called upon him in the night, He might want to take him by the hand, so he thought he had better leave it outside the sheets so as to be ready!

Our sloppy modern sentimentalists, who mentally wallow in the bathos of jazz jeremiads, and so-called "spirituals," whined by unmanly foreign musical directors in night clubs and hotels, will see nothing beautiful in such a story, but as very few of them are likely to read this biography, or to have any appreciation of the works of Lewis Carroll, that is of very small moment.

CHAPTER XI

LEWIS CARROLL'S PLACE AS THE FOUNDER OF "NONSENSE LITERATURE."

IN considering the various qualities which have made the name of Lewis Carroll immortal, it must be conceded that, like the majority of those who have achieved lasting reputation in English literature, he was "born with a silver spoon in his mouth," in respect of possessing parents able and eager to give him a University education of a kind sufficient to enable him to secure a well-paid, comfortable, gentlemanly and permanent occupation, and thus render him independent of any necessity to write for his living. I wonder how many of our great writers of the calibre of Milton, Dryden, Byron, Shelley, Keats (for even he had a small private income) and Tennyson, among the poets, and Scott, Lamb, Macaulay, Thackeray and Lytton, to name a few among the prose writers, would have remained "mute inglorious Miltons" if, like Burns, Dickens, Francis Thompson, and our present-day "provocateur" of paradox and brilliant Hibernian blarney, they had possessed nothing except their talent with which to conquer the snobbish goddess, Fame. And how many of our leading living poets and essayists could have risen out of the rut of mediocrity if they had not possessed safe jobs, as deans or dons, or Government officials, which permitted them to woo Fame instead of having to fight her ?

Without such security, or that of private means, the end of any of the literary luminosities of the past I have mentioned might well have been that of Thomas Chatterton, whose talent was not less than that of his more fortunately-born contemporary Walpole, for critics [1] and connoisseurs, with hardly an exception, have ever been apathetic when creative ability has lacked influence, or the freedom from material anxieties which is almost, though fortunately not quite, indispensable to literary opportunity. I myself have known at least one such poet who, given the opportunity of the fortunate poets I have mentioned, would assuredly have been recognised as a master, and I dare wager that there is not a literary man of any deep and varied experience who would not endorse my reflections.

It must also be conceded that Lewis Carroll, like all the Victorian writers, lived in the "golden age of literature," in respect of general opportunity and the appreciation of the reading public. There were no cinemas to allure this public with glittering drivel, concocted by Hebraic coteries in Hollywood,

[1] In this connection, I remember the late Arnold Bennett telling me with regret that with reference to his own literary criticisms he had no voice in the selection of authors or books, the choice, in every case, being made by his employers who, quite apart from any of the "influences" I have enumerated, might reasonably be expected to favour those authors whose publishers rented the most advertising space.

to excite and stultify the brain; no vast syndicates exploiting hundreds of trashy sentimental or sensational weekly journals, edited by ex-office boys, and designed to serve what these literary mechanics and their managing directors, in the jargon of the trade, call the "mill girl public," and no broadcasting monopolists to make further competition for the leisure hours of the populace with discussions and discordances, and reviews by society critics of the works of society authors.

Life in the great cities was almost entirely unhampered by the continual threats, or performances, of elections and strikes and the clash of creeds and classes this involves to-day, and for the majority of people it flowed on smoothly and uneventfully. Our fathers loved, and laboured, or idled, with a freedom from worry and excitement which may not have been very stimulating, but must have added much to the amenities of life.

As a result, the classes and masses alike were interested to turn to "something different" in their literary and theatrical recreations, and not only were "Hamlet" and "Macbeth," and other tragedies of Shakespeare, indubitably more popular than his comedies, and numbers of touring and "stock" companies enabled to play them profitably for years, but mournful and maudlin melodrama of the "East Lynne" variety formed the staple food of most theatrical bills of fare outside of the West End of London, and comedy—which in these days of worry and insecurity is naturally preferred by all save the small minority who lead safe or sheltered lives—had, definitely, to take second place.

It says more, therefore, for Lewis Carroll's unique qualities that he should have achieved immediate fame as a literary humorist during such an era, than that his works should enjoy universal popularity to-day, when humour has become a necessary antidote to the general infestivity of life.

But although to-day we abound in humorists, few of them seem to have studied the technique and requirements of comedy, as it was studied and understood by those founders of most forms of artistic expression, the Greeks, whose comic work, according to no less an authority than Schlegel, was entirely gay and mirthful and formed a complete contrast to their tragedy.

Lewis Carroll's best work is wholly of this order and, as I shall presently show, for all his seeming spontaneity he was essentially a conscious and responsible jester, who possessed in a high degree that "infinite capacity for taking pains" which sages in all ages appear to have considered one of the most important constituents of genius.

But his claim to greatness rests not upon this, or upon the fact that he has written a couple of books which will remain classics for all time, but upon the much greater achievement of having founded a school of literary endeavour.

Before the advent of "Alice in Wonderland," literary creation and thought had no other idea of nonsense than as a general label for nursery rhyme humour, or as a contemptuous term to classify unintentional absurdity, such as that ridiculed by Macaulay in his famous essay on the poems of Robert Montgomery. Here and there a few writers of repute had timorously ventured down nonsense byways, only to return before they had traversed more than a few yards of the unaccustomed road and resume their activities on ground which was more familiar to them.

Aristophanes in "The Knights," Shakespeare in "A Midsummer Night's Dream," Bishop Corbett in the early seventeenth century, Oliver Goldsmith and Samuel Johnson, were all such experimenters, and, in later days, Charles Lamb, Shirley Brooks, Thackeray and Oliver Wendell Holmes; but their endeavours (Shakespeare's excepted) altogether lacked the charm and resource of Carroll, and Thackeray's nonsense ballad, "Little Billee," now deservedly forgotten, is probably the most execrable composition of its kind ever perpetrated.

Even Edward Lear and Stuart Calverley, both of whom could write excellent nonsense verse, did not regard their talent in this direction half as seriously as they did their very ordinary ability at more classical and more recognised forms of artistic expression, and it was not until the former made an unexpected success with the third-rate limericks in his "Book of Nonsense,"[1] that he

---

[1] Which was a success not through any outstanding merit but because it was the *first* book of its kind and had no competition of any sort to encounter.

appears to have given the writing of nonsense any particular consideration.

It has remained for Lewis Carroll to raise the writing of nonsense to a literary art and to establish it as a recognised form of Anglo-Saxon[1] humour. For this reason, if for no other, he would deserve his place among the immortals, and had Sir Walter Besant revised his standard work, "The French Humourists From the Twelfth to the Nineteenth Century" (1873), a score of years after publication, he could hardly have failed to have made acknowledgement of this in his final paragraph, which emphasises his belief in the superiority of the French humorists over those of Great Britain, thus:

> "Rabelais has, I maintain, a finer wit than Swift; we have no political satire so good as the 'Satyr Menippe,' we have no early British humour compatible for a moment with that of the Jabliaux, we have no letter-writer like Voltaire, we have no teller of tales like La Fontaine and, lastly, we have no chansonier like Beranger."

All this may be true; I am not competent to endorse it or to deny it, but I do not think that any student of literature, in this country or abroad, will quarrel with me for asserting that neither France nor any other country has produced a writer of nonsense who can be compared with Lewis Carroll, or (I might add) a writer of travesty who can be mentioned in the same breath with

---

[1] I thus include James Whitcomb Riley and other delightful nonsense writers of America.

W. S. Gilbert. The latter, despite his "Yarn of the Nancy Bell," cannot strictly be regarded as a writer of nonsense, but he shares with his Christ Church contemporary that talent for polite and exquisite humour, expressed in uncommon phraseology, which charms the ear (when recited or read) no less than it does the heart and mind.

With regard to nonsense literature, which, thanks to the subject of this biography, has now become a recognised department of authorship, it is strange that none of the compilers of the various dictionaries of literary terms appear to have attempted any sort of definition. In endeavouring to supply this deficiency, I am conscious of the responsibility of my task, and, therefore, it is with some trepidation that I shall commence the next chapter with some explication of the standard I have set up for my own guidance when adventuring in Nonsense Land.

CHAPTER XII

"NONSENSE" is the apotheosis of the preposterous. Its conscious humour is based either upon absurd and incongruous action on the part of its principal characters, upon the paradoxical and eccentric use of words and phrases, of the precise meaning of which their adaptor has the most accurate conception, or upon a coined vocabulary of which the words, although ludicrous to the eye and ear, are, essentially, onomatopoetic. It may be parodic and even lightly ironic, but it is never satiric and very rarely contains a moral. When a moral does occur, as in the case of that ballad of bivalvular victimisation, "The Walrus and the Carpenter," with its warning to the young and guileless not to trust to soft-spoken strangers, it is intended to be a subsidiary effect in the whole design.

In considering the qualities in Lewis Carroll's works which most delight and amuse us, we have first to realise that he is only superficially a writer for children. I was offered an amusing instance of this not long ago, during the discussion which

Tenniel's Drawing of Humpty Dumpty

followed my reading a paper on Lewis Carroll to
my fellow members of that unobtrusive but vener-
able literary society the Casual Club. An Aus-
tralian member related how, some twenty years
previously, in Queensland, he had purchased a
copy of "Alice in Wonderland" as a birthday
present for a small niece and had become so
fascinated with the story himself that he bought
another copy for his own library. A few days later
he received a letter from his little relative in which
she said she wished he had given her a book that
grown-ups did not care for, as "daddy has become
so fond of it that he has taken it to business with
him and I haven't had a chance to read it"!

Children, of course, enjoy Lewis Carroll's fun
and fantasy as much as their elders, but only the
latter can appreciate his background of gentle
irony and his ingenious parodies on poems and
phrases. Most of his rhymes in the "Alice" and
"Sylvie and Bruno" books are of this order. Two
examples from "Through the Looking Glass" are
the White Knight's Song, which is a skit on
Wordsworth's "Resolution and Independence,"[1]
and the song to Alice, commencing "To the

[1] In the first version of the parody, which was published in "The Train,"
in 1856, under the title of "The Lonely Man," he admits this. The opening verse was then as follows:

I met an aged, aged man,
  Upon the lonely moor;
I knew I was a gentleman,
  And he was but a boor.
So I stopped and roughly questioned him,
  "Come tell me where you live?"
But his words impressed my ear no more
  Than if it was a sieve.

Looking Glass World it was Alice that Said," which is, of course, a parody of Scott's "Bonny Dundee." Probably the most fascinating characteristics in Lewis Carroll's writings are his intangibility and incompleteness. His quaint conversations and fantastic scenes abound in ideas which seem to vanish like the Cheshire Cat—leaving only the smile behind, or like our indeterminate conception of his immortal Snark, that was not strictly a Snark because it was a Boojum!

He never makes the mistake of less responsible and less designing writers of satiating us with good things; on completing a story by him, we are always left with the impression that, had he felt so disposed, he could have added another chapter or two which would have proved equally alluring.

And, more than any other writer, he has fathomed the mysterious depths of childhood that lie within us—even within the hearts of those of us who are but children of a larger growth. He could see the Divinity which lies behind the smile of an innocent child, and the magic of his personality was such that his little friends trusted him with their childish secrets in perfect confidence, and were inspired to feel for him an affection which was equally compounded of comradeship and reverence.

It is these propensities, together with his command of language and "technique"—noticeable even when his imagination and fancy run at their most preposterous riot—which surely provide the answer to the question as to what are the constituent factors responsible for Lewis Carroll's popularity; and I disagree emphatically with the opinion in an anthology compiled not long ago by a distinguished and charming foreign writer[1] who considers that "the poetry of nonsense, as Carroll understood it, is entirely irresponsible, and the main point about it is that there is no point."

This gentleman has, like many others, I venture to think, made the mistake of regarding Lewis Carroll from a literal point of view, instead of a literary one, for such a description, if correct, would reduce his work to the level of the "eenar deenar dinar doe" gibberish of the nursery, or to the unconscious nonsense babblings of idiocy. To carry the argument still further, any combination of words picked haphazard from the dictionary might be called a nonsense story!

I agree that legitimate nonsense verse and prose appear to be entirely irresponsible, but surely that is one of the phases of paradox which makes the fantasies of Carroll and Barrie, and F. W. Thomas[2] so charming to every individual between nine and ninety who retains anything of the divine spark of childhood within his heart, whether he realises the reason for his enchantment or not.

Actually the nonsense writings of Lewis Carroll are a highly technical form of conscious and responsible humour which, when analysed, are found to contain plot (or "idea"), achievement,

[1] Monsieur Emile Cammaerts.
[2] Who has no greater admirer than myself.

climax and, in the case of his poems, rhyme and rhythm. "Jabberwocky" affords excellent proof of this. Rhyme and rhythm, indeed, are essential to good nonsense verse, which the further removed it is from the rules of sense must conform the more closely to rules of sound! It is these factors, and the others I have mentioned in connection with them, which render nonsense verse so superior to the nonsense rhymes of the nursery and the folk song, including the sea chanty. One type is nonsense, the other d—— nonsense. Then, of course, there is sheer nonsense; but as this is principally confined to the speeches and writings of politicians, I need not enlarge on that variety here.

So responsible and conscious a literary jester was Lewis Carroll that it is doubtful whether there has ever been a more meticulous precisian in the use and intentional misuse of words, including those coined by himself.

In the preface to "The Hunting of the Snark," he gives the most exact directions as to the pronunciation of the outlandish words in that perfect nonsense ballad, "Jabberwocky," and whimsically complains against the human perversity of people who try to pronounce the first "o" in "borogroves" like that of the "o" in "worry," instead of the first "o" in "borrow," while his instructions as to the pronunciation of "frumious," though not altogether free from the suspicion of "leg-pulling," are equally unequivocal. Says he, "Make up your mind that you will say both 'fuming' and 'furious,' but leave it unsettled which you will say first. Now open your mouth and speak. If your thoughts incline ever so little towards 'fuming' you will say 'fuming-furious,' if they turn, by even a hair's breadth towards 'furious,' you will say 'furious-fuming,' but if you have that rarest of gifts, a perfectly balanced mind, you will say 'frumious.'"

Could any adjective sound more appropriate to a creature bearing so menacing a name as "Bandersnatch"? "Frumious," is, of course, a "portmanteau-word,"[1] the meaning of which, as defined by Lewis Carroll is one word with two meanings packed into it. "Mimsy," meaning flimsy and miserable, another portmanteau-word, seems singularly suitable to the "borogrove," an ornithological freak described by Humpty Dumpty as being "a thin, shabby-looking bird with its feathers sticking all round—something like a live mop," while yet another example, "slithy," meaning lithe and slimy, seems entirely applicable when used in connection with "toves," creatures described by Humpty Dumpty as being "something like lizards, something like badgers and something like corkscrews, who make their nests under sun-dials and live on cheese."

Apart from Carroll's insistence on pronunciation and meaning, every word and every punctuation mark had to be printed exactly as he had planned

---

[1] Here again, our ingenious droll has invented a fashion in words which has been followed by subsequent humorists. Probably the best-known post-Carroll example is that popular portmanteau-word "brunch," meaning a meal taken between breakfast and lunch.

in his development of the spontaneous idea upon which the particular story or poem was based, and no author took more trouble to ensure that the illustrations in his books corresponded exactly to his conception of the subjects. Thus, in "Sylvie and Bruno Concluded," appears an announcement which states:

"For over twenty-five years I have made it my chief object, with regard to my books, that they should be of the best workmanship obtainable at the price. And I am deeply annoyed to find that the last issue of 'Through the Looking Glass,' consisting of the Sixtieth Thousand, has been put on sale without it being noticed that most of the pictures have failed so much in the printing as to make the book not worth buying. I request all holders of copies to send them to Messrs. ———— (the publishers) with their names and addresses, and copies of the new issue shall be sent them in exchange."

At the risk of making an anti-climax to the chapter I will state that, conscious and designed though Lewis Carroll's literary humour was, his verbal humour was often as spontaneous and effective as Dr. Johnson's. As an illustration of this, Major Dodgson has related to me an incident which took place on an occasion when he and his distinguished relative were crossing Tom Quad, one Sunday morning, after having listened to rather a dull sermon preached in the University Church by Dr. Stubbs, who afterwards became a Bishop.[1] They encountered the preacher, and as it was drizzling with rain Lewis Carroll politely offered

[1] Of Chester.

the loan of his umbrella, to be met with the rather ungracious remark: "No thanks. I don't mind getting wet; in fact I like getting wet!"

"You were dry enough in the pulpit this morning!" retorted the author of "Alice in Wonderland" gravely, as he hurried away with his nephew before the other cleric had time to think of a suitable reply.

CHAPTER XIII

THE STRANGE CASE OF PROFESSOR DODGSON AND MR. CARROLL—THE VIEWS OF TENNIEL AND FURNISS ON THEM—COMPLAINING TO CARROLL ABOUT DODGSON!—HOW THE FORMER GOT HIS IDEAS.

UNDOUBTEDLY Lewis Carroll had his limitations, and in saying this I do not refer to the work published under the name of C. L. Dodgson, with which I am very little concerned. When he attempted to be deliberately and continuously serious he was often mediocre, particularly when he endeavoured to combine theological and political controversy and a love romance (one of the most "penny-novelettish" ever penned) with nonsense, as in the "Sylvie and Bruno" books, which I defy anyone to read right through without weariness of mind and vexation of spirit.

And there is strong indication that he intended to carry his incursions into the more commonplace land of "Common Sense" still further, for in the preface to one of these books he has referred to his desire to produce a series of improving books, including a Child's Bible, a scriptural anthology, and a Shakespeare for girls. The last was to exclude everything not suitable for the perusal of girls from ten to seventeen. All admirable projects in their way, but ones which could have been equally well developed by almost any well-read person of average literary ability and very little imagination. For a creative writer of rare and exquisite fancy to occupy his mind with them, to the exclusion of original work, is rather like a great artist designing a series of frames for somebody else's paintings.

It is more than probable that such collaboration between Lewis Carroll and C. L. Dodgson—for that is what it would have amounted to—would have proved no more felicitous than their co-operation in the "Sylvie and Bruno" books. Their temperaments were so different that I doubt if even the famous case of the Duke of Portland and Mr. Druce offers a stranger or more interesting instance of dual personality. That which is said to have affected William Cowper seems to have been much less developed.

Mr. Carroll, boyish, whimsical, eager, reciprocal, sociable, fond of recognition[1] and intensely human; and Professor Dodgson, serious, donnish, mature, shy, aloof, introspective, egotistic, easily-offended and displaying very little interest in other adult people, including Mr. Carroll, with whom he almost invariably disclaimed relationship. The latter repaid him by never mentioning Mr. Dodgson in any of his books.

[1] Probably no author ever presented so many copies of his works. Apart from the very many inscribed copies which he gave to friends and mere acquaintances, and to complete strangers; thousands were distributed to the children's hospitals.

Other people might confound the twain, including Queen Victoria,[1] but the droll and the don, however friendly they might be when they associated in the privacy of the study—and here, too, one suspects they had many differences of opinion—had so little in common that they declined to recognise one another in public. A friend of both, "W.H.D.", in a tiny memoir written in 1907, recalled how in 1884, when he was stopping in the house of a mutual friend, a parson in the Midlands:

"there came to call a certain genial and by no means shy Dean, who, without realising what he was doing, proceeded in the presence of other callers to make some remark identifying Mr. Dodgson as the author of his books. There followed an immense explosion immediately on the visitor's departure, with a pathetic and serious request that, if there were any risk of a repetition of the call, due warning might be given and the retreat secured."

It is possible that Professor Dodgson's attitude may have been influenced by the rather flippant though very entertaining way in which Mr. Carroll treated his many attempts to collaborate by introducing little mathematical problems. On the various occasions Mr. Carroll did include such arithmetical interpolations in his stories and verses, he dealt with them logically and correctly enough, but in a spirit of facetiousness which must have

[1] Her Majesty, being charmed with "Alice in Wonderland," and being informed by some materialistic advisor that the author was the Rev. C. L. Dodgson, ordered the rest of his works, only to receive a parcel of mathematical and theological publications.

A TIFF WITH TENNIEL   129

been rather disturbing to the mathematical mind of his other self. In "Phantasmagoria" he even made a verse out of an equation![1] In "A Tangled Tale," Mr. Dodgson was allowed more latitude than usual, and the result of this mistaken kindness on the part of Mr. Carroll was not wholly satisfactory.

My suggestion that Carroll and Dodgson were, in effect, two different personalities inhabiting one body may not appear so fantastic, even to readers who pride themselves on their plain common sense, or to near relatives whose disbelief in such a theory is founded upon their recollections that no such division of personality was apparent in the family circle,[2] if I quote some remarkable evidence endorsing it, which I did not discover until I had already set down my views on the matter. I came across it in an article on Lewis Carroll which appeared in the "Strand Magazine[3]" in 1908. It was written by the late Harry Furniss, who illustrated the "Sylvie and Bruno" books, and the famous *Punch* artist not only supports my dual identity theory but my long-held belief as to the designed and conscious humour of Carroll also.

According to Mr. Furniss, Sir John Tenniel refused to illustrate any more of Lewis Carroll's works after "Through the Looking Glass," and held very unfavourable views on what he called the "pretentiousness" and "obstinacy" of the

[1] See "Four Riddles" at the end of that book.
[2] One of his closest relatives has, however, expressed to me his implicit belief in it.
[3] To the publishers of which, Messrs. George Newnes, Ltd., I am indebted for permission to make the required quotations.

I

Dodgson part of him. When he heard that Furniss was proposing to illustrate "Sylvie and Bruno," he warned him in the following words: "I'll give you a week, old chap; you will never be able to put up with the fellow any longer. He is impossible!"

As an example of this alleged "impossibility," it may be mentioned that "Through the Looking Glass" originally contained a passage, not in the published version, which introduced a wasp in a wig, presumably in the character of a judge or barrister. This was too much for Tenniel, who complained in a letter that "a wasp in a wig is altogether beyond the appliances of art."

But Tenniel was a poor prophet, as the following testimony by Furniss proves:

"We worked together for seven years, and a kindlier man than Lewis Carroll never existed. Dodgson, the arithmetician, was less acceptable. He subjected every illustration, when finished, to a minute examination under the magnifying glass. He would take a square inch of the drawing, count the lines I had made in that space and compare their number with those in a square inch of illustration for 'Alice' made by Tenniel!

"And, in due course, I would receive a long essay on the subject from Dodgson the mathematician.[1] Naturally this led to disagreements, particularly when it came to foreshortening a figure, which is a question for the eye and not for the foot rule and compass. In fact, over the criticism of one drawing I pretended that I would stand Dodgson the Don no longer and wrote to Carroll declining to complete the work.

"Mr. Dodgson was undoubtedly hard to please; he told me that with the exception of Humpty Dumpty he did not like Tenniel's drawings. It was lucky for him

[1] The seventy odd letters comprising the correspondence between the author and the artist were sold by auction in New York, in 1930.

that he found an artist in John Tenniel exactly suitable for him, for in spite of what he said, Tenniel's work for 'Alice' did nearly as much to make it a success as Carroll's originality.

"His humour was not spontaneous; in himself[1] he was a dull man, his jokes, elaborate and designed were feeble. He had a peculiar twist in his brain that gave his mathematical mind a bent towards some humorous line of thought, taking him he knew not where, and why he could not say. He himself confessed as much:

"'I was walking on a hillside, alone, one bright summer day,' he told me, 'when suddenly there came into my head one line of verse, one solitary line: "For the Snark *was* a Boojum, you see!" I knew not what it meant then. I do not know what it means now, but I wrote it down, and some time afterwards, the rest of the stanza occurred to me, that being its last line, and so by degrees, at odd moments during the next year or two, the rest of the poem pieced itself together, that being its last stanza.'

"Again: 'I distinctly remember how, in a desperate attempt to strike out some new line of fairy-lore, I had sent my heroine straight down a rabbit hole, to begin with, without the least notion of what was going to happen afterwards. And so, to please a child I loved (I don't remember having any other motive) I printed[2] the manuscript and illustrated with my own crude designs—designs that rebelled against every law of anatomy and art (for I had never had a lesson in drawing) —the book which was later reproduced in facsimile.[3]

"'In writing it out, I added many fresh ideas, which seemed to grow of themselves upon the original stock; and many more added themselves when, years afterwards, I wrote it all out again for publication; but (and this may interest some readers of "Alice" to know) every word of the dialogue *came of itself*.

"'Sometimes an idea comes at night, when I have to get up and write it down—sometimes when out on a

[1] I.e., as Mr. Dodgson. Obviously he was very far from being dull company when, inspired by children, he became Mr. Carroll, as the reminiscences of his former child friends, quoted in this biography, prove.

[2] He refers to the copy made in script-hand for Alice Liddell, not to the manuscript for publication.

[3] I.e., published.

lonely winter walk, when I have had to stop, and with half frozen fingers, jot down a few words which would keep the new-born idea from perishing—but whenever and however it comes, it comes of *itself*. I cannot write as though I were a clock, by being wound up, nor do I believe that any original writer could so produce.'

"Lewis Carroll's work did not end with his writing, or even with the illustrations. He saw to the publication as well—not so much, I imagine, in a commercial as in an artistic sense. He paid for everything, and the books were published for him on the usual trade commission."

In "Confessions of a Caricaturist," the entertaining book of reminiscences by Mr. Furniss which was published in 1891, the genial artist sketches an even more complete pen picture of Mr. Dodgson, as follows:

"He was not selfish, but a liberal-minded, open-handed philanthropist; but his egotism was all but second childhood. He informed my wife that she was the most privileged woman in the world, for she knew the man who knew his (Lewis Carroll's) ideas—that ought to comfort her! She must not *see* a picture or read a line of the MS, it was sufficient for her to gaze at me outside of my studio with admiration and respect, as the only man, besides Lewis Carroll himself, with a knowledge of the latter's works. Furthermore, he sent me an elaborate document to sign committing myself to secrecy.

"This I indignantly refused to sign. 'My word is as good as my bond,' I said, and striking an attitude I hinted that I would strike, inasmuch as I would not work for years isolated from my wife and friends. I was allowed to show my wife the drawings.

"But his egotism carried him still further. He was determined no one should read his MS but he and I, so in the dead of night; he cut his MS into horizontal strips of four or five lines, then placed the whole of it in a sack and shook it up; taking out a piece by piece, he pasted the sheets down as they happened to come. These disconnected strips were elaborately and mysteriously marked with numbers and letters and various hieroglyphics, to decipher which would have turned my assumed eccentricity into positive madness. I therefore sent the whole MS back to him again and threatened to strike! This had the desired effect. I received an MS I could read."

Incidentally, it may be mentioned that for the models of his drawings of the fairy children in the "Sylvie and Bruno" books, Mr. Furniss used his own children.

Mrs. Isa Barclay, and others quoted in this biography, have also shown that there existed a very real difference between Carroll and Dodgson, and other useful testimony to the frigid and un-Carroll-like nature of the latter may be found among the series of letters with reference to Lewis Carroll published in "The Times" during the end of December, 1931, of which the following, written by Sir Herbert Maxwell, is an example:

"Dimly through the mist of sixty-eight years does your leading article about Lewis Carroll bring before me the lean, dark-haired person of Charles Lutwidge Dodgson, before whom, as mathematical lecturer, we undergraduates of Christ Church used to assemble. Very few, if any, of my contemporaries survive to confirm my impression of the singularly dry and perfunctory manner in which he imparted instruction to us, never betraying the slightest personal interest in matters that were of deep concern to us. Yet this must have been the very time when he was framing the immortal fantasia of Alice."

"The abysmal deeps of personality," as Tennyson calls them, are certainly difficult to fathom!

CHAPTER XIV

LEWIS CARROLL AND AMERICA—THE RECORD
SALE OF THE "ALICE" MANUSCRIPT—"ALICE"
ON THE CINEMA SCREEN—EPITAPH.

IT would be unfair, as well as grossly neglectful,
to conclude this biography without grateful
reference to the admiration expressed for the
works of Lewis Carroll in the United States, where
I am assured that a large proportion of the children
of Anglo-Saxon stock are "brought-up" on the
"Alice" books, and that the writings of their
creator are considered such classics that most of
his original manuscripts, including the family magazines he edited when a boy, have been acquired
by the Library of Harvard College!

It is, I suppose, much too much to hope that
the University of Oxford, where Lewis Carroll
spent more than forty years of his working life,
will, in the near future, offer retaliation in the
true Carollian spirit of topsy-turvydom by acquiring,
for preservation in the famous Bodleian Library,
some of the original manuscripts of a great American
humorist, such as Mark Twain!

After such recognition it seems the most natural
thing in the world that the original manuscript of
"Alice" should have become one of America's

Chapter 1

Alice was beginning to get very tired of sitting by her sister on the bank, and of having nothing to do: once or twice she had peeped into the book her sister was reading, but it had no pictures or conversations in it, and where is the use of a book, thought Alice, without pictures or conversations? So she was considering in her own mind, (as well as she could, for the hot day made her feel very sleepy and stupid,) whether the pleasure of making a daisy-chain was worth the trouble of getting up and picking the daisies, when a white rabbit with pink eyes ran close by her.

There was nothing very remarkable in that, nor did Alice think it so _very_ much out of the way to hear the rabbit say to itself "dear, dear! I shall be too late!" (when she thought it over afterwards, it occurred to her that she ought to have wondered at this, but at the time it all seemed quite natural); but when the rabbit actually took a watch out of its waistcoat-pocket, looked at it, and then hurried on, Alice started to her feet, for

THE FIRST TWO PAGES OF THE ORIGINAL "ALICE" MS.

A Christmas Gift
to
a Dear Child
in Memory
of
'a Summer Day.

most cherished literary treasures, and that an official handbook issued, a few years ago, by the American National Union of Students should have recommended the study of "Alice in Wonderland" as calculated to give young Americans some comprehension of English life and thought, and why, also, so many American visitors make the toilsome pilgrimage to Old Guildford Cemetery, almost on the summit of the "Hog's Back," to pay tribute before the unpretentious tomb with the plain white cross and pediment. Of this I have been personally assured by the aged sexton, who not only buried Charles Lutwidge Dodgson but was acquainted with him and with Lewis Carroll.

This Transatlantic devotion goes far to explain the unprecedented scene which occurred in Sotheby's famous auction rooms, London, on April 22nd, 1929, when the original manuscript of the story told to the three Liddell sisters and subsequently (between July, 1862, and February, 1863) set down in writing and presented to sweet Alice Liddell, was offered for auction by her adult self, Mrs. Reginald P. Hargreaves, in the presence of an enthusiastic crowd, who filled the large auction room and overflowed into the passages and corridors long before the sale commenced. Among the interesting people present I noticed Mr. John Burns, Sir Frederick Kenyon (who represented the British Museum), and, of course, the original Alice.

The manuscript, beautifully written in script form, consisted of 92 pages only (each 7⅜ inches by 4½ inches and containing about 240 words), and in addition to its ornamental title page was illustrated with 37 pen and ink sketches by the author and a photograph, taken by him, of Alice Liddell, pasted at the foot of the last page. The whole manuscript contained, approximately, 22,000 words, or a quarter the length of an average novel.

The bidding for this tiny treasure started at £5,000 and soon rose to £12,500, when Mr. Dring, of the firm of Quaritch, retired, leaving the field to three competitors—the auctioneer, who was bidding for Mr. Gabriel Wells, of New York, a gentleman named Maggs, and Dr. A. S. W. Rosenbach of Philadelphia, who is possibly the world's greatest authority on Britain's literary treasures, a paradox which is certainly in the true spirit of "Alice." I regret I am unable to match it by reference to an Englishman whose knowledge of America's literary treasures exceeds that of anyone in the New World.

The British Museum made no bid of any kind, and in conversation with an official of that institution, who was present at the sale, I gathered that the trustees, although desirous of purchasing the manuscript, had no funds available for a bid higher than £2,000.

Mr. Maggs withdrew from the contest at £14,500, as did the auctioneer at £15,200, and at £15,400, amid a scene of much excitement, the MS went to Dr. Rosenbach. He told me afterwards that he came prepared to pay £20,000, had that been necessary.

The price paid constitutes an auction "record" for a book in Great Britain, and is actually £2,500 more than was realised by a first folio Shakespeare.

Dr. Rosenbach also secured a copy of the second edition of "Alice in Wonderland" (1866), inscribed "Alice Pleasance Liddell, from the author," which went at £1,500; and a copy of the first edition printed at Oxford in 1865, presented and inscribed by the author to Mrs. Craik, author of "John Halifax, Gentleman," which realised £5,000.

It is only fair to add that both Dr. Rosenbach and the American underbidder, Mr. Gabriel Wells (had he been successful) were prepared to re-sell the MS to the British Museum without profit; indeed the former generously offered to contribute five hundred guineas towards such a purchase.

But with all our gold in America, as part of the price we paid for the privilege of being permitted to play the principal part in "making the world safe for democracy," it was inevitable that the "Alice" manuscript should also find a home there. With Dr. Rosenbach's other "Alice" prizes, it was purchased by Mr. Eldridge R. Johnson, of New Jersey, for a sum exceeding £30,000. Later, this gentleman loaned the manuscript for exhibition to the State Libraries of America. At the Free Library of Philadelphia alone more than 400,000 people inspected it during the fourteen weeks following the end of June, 1929.

Such wholesale devotion on the part of America to a British author, whose humour is essentially English, suggests that, after all, there must be something basically sound in the traditional cousin-ship of the two nations, however much Hibernian writers of unintentional nonsense may affect to sneer at the suggestion as mere sentimentality.

A paradoxical perplexity of America's admiration —I had almost said veneration—for Lewis Carroll is the fact that she should have permitted her cinema screens, and those of Great Britain, to be infested with an execrable talking version of "Alice in Wonderland," concocted in Hollywood in 1931 by a gang of iconoclasts who so little understood the true spirit of "Alice" that they permitted her sophisticated little representative to "make eyes" at the Knave of Hearts, and to say of the White Rabbit, in pronounced Bowery accents, "Isn't he cute?" And to add insult to injury, in the exploita-tion and publicity sheets which they issued with the film to the American cinema exhibitors, they referred to the author of "Alice in Wonderland" as Sir Lewis Carroll! Had I not seen one of these remarkable papers, which contained other aston-ishing biographical errors, I should have doubted that such ignorance could have prevailed—even in Hollywood—about a man who has become one of the literary idols of the United States.

In contrast to this contemptible effort I saw, in April, 1930, a film ballet in colours of "Through the Looking Glass," with which I could find no fault, although it was made in Hollywood and, paradoxically enough, was interpolated into a very poor picture of American vaudeville life with the stupid title of "Puttin' on the Ritz." Mr. Edward H. Sloman, the English director of this ballet had, I imagine, been given an absolutely free hand, for he had contrived to exclude from it those tiresome accessories of "pep" and "punch" which render so many American films tedious to most people whose intelligence is much above that possessed by an earwig, with the result that it was entirely charming and entertaining. The accompanying music of Irving Berlyn was equally delightful and in the true spirit of Carroll, and the same can be said of Joan Bennett's performance of Alice, and of the impersonations of the artists who represented the weird creatures who peopled her strange world, who all looked exactly like Tenniel's drawings, and moved with a strange and fantastic grace that suggested nothing human.

I endeavoured to persuade the London agents of the producers to allow this delightful ballet to be freed from the dull film in which it was imprisoned, and exhibited as a special Christmas entertainment (which would assuredly have "drawn" all London) but was met with the reply that their principals in Hollywood would not allow it to be shown apart from the longer picture!

If we have not reciprocated America's appreciation of Lewis Carroll with an equally intense and comprehensive admiration for any specific American writer, O. Henry, at any rate, has become a classic among us, and probably most of us, whose reading extends beyond the works of Mr. Edgar Wallace and the film "fan" journals, would consider him the World's Best Short Story Writer, despite the popularity of the engrossing but much less charming and less entertaining Guy de Maupassant.

Such lovely spirits as Carroll and O. Henry are better ambassadors for Anglo-American friendship and understanding than any which could be provided by the Diplomatic Service of either country, for their propaganda work is infinite. Men like these need no monuments of state to keep alive their fame, which is sufficiently commemorated by the sentiment expressed in St. Paul's Cathedral, concerning its architect: "Si momentum requiris, circumspice."

Nevertheless, when little Denmark can honour Hans Christian Andersen by constructing a Memorial Park in her capital, containing statues of his best-known characters set among leafy bowers and flower gardens, and Llandudno and Darlington[1] can indicate their remote connection with Lewis Carroll with memorials, it seems strange that the house in which the physical complement of him died is not even distinguished by a plaque. Perhaps Mr. Eldridge Johnson, or Dr. Rosenbach, or some other American Carroll lover may

[1] A "house" in the Darlington Girls' High School is named after Lewis Carroll, in memory of his connection with Croft Spa. The badge of the Carroll House is the White Knight of "Through the Looking Glass."

read these lines and shame us by rectifying this omission.

To the other memorials, there seems every probability there will shortly be added a "Lewis Carroll Ward for Children," at St. Mary's Hospital, Paddington, London, as the result of a letter published in the newspapers from a Carroll devotee suggesting such a centenary commemoration. A committee of enthusiastic and eminent people has been formed to give effect to the proposal, and by the time these lines are in print it probably will have assumed definite form.

That Lewis Carroll foresaw something of the imperishable appeal of his dream child, and even planned it, is suggested by these strangely prophetic lines in the epilogistic poem to "Through the Looking Glass":

> Still she haunts me phantomwise,
> Alice moving under skies,
> Never seen by mortal eyes.
>
> Children yet, the tale to hear,
> Eager eye and willing ear,
> Lovingly shall nestle near.

And in the letter to "every child who loves Alice," which concludes both "Alice" books, occurs the following paragraph:

"If I have written anything to add to those stories of innocent and healthy amusement that are laid up in books for the children I love so well, it is surely something I may hope to look back upon without shame and sorrow (as how much of life must then be recalled) when *my* turn comes to walk through the valley of the shadows."

If an epitaph be required to mark the centenary year of Lewis Carroll, what could be more appropriate than this?

THE END